The Beauty of Dogs

The Beauty of Dogs

Edited by Arthur Wyngate
Photography by Robert & Eunice Pearcy

JG PRESS

Published in the USA 1995 by JG Press
Distributed by World Publications, Inc.

The JG Press imprint is a trademark of JG Press, Inc.
455 Somerset Avenue
North Dighton, MA 02764

Produced by
Brompton Books Corporation
15 Sherwood Place
Greenwich, Connecticut 06830

Copyright © 1995 Brompton Books Corporation

All rights reserved. No part of this publication may be reproduced, stored in a retrieval system or transmitted in any form by any means, electronic, mechanical, photocopying or otherwise, without first obtaining the written permission of the copyright owner.

ISBN 1-57215-087-4

Printed in China

Edited and captioned by Bill Yenne
Designed by Ruth DeJauregui

Page 1: A cute puppy with apparent retriever breeding.
Page 2: First cousin to the Collie, the Shetland Sheepdog is a popular herding breed.
Below: The Golden Retriever is an energetic, well-tempered and extremely popular breed.

Photo Credits:
All photographs copyright © Robert and Eunice Pearcy.

CONTENTS

INTRODUCTION
6

THE ORIGIN OF THE DOG
14

CHOOSING A DOG
24

TERRIERS
36

HOUNDS
52

WORKING AND HERDING DOGS
64

TOYS
88

SPORTING DOGS
102

NON-SPORTING BREEDS
114

INDEX
128

INTRODUCTION

The dog is one of the most beautiful of all creatures, and as a species, the dog's beauty is further underscored by the wondrous variety among its breeds. Dogs may be large or small; their coats may be luxuriously long or smooth and sleek; they may be bred as hunters or merely for show. Whatever the case, they also have much in common, from the warmth and intelligence conveyed in their eyes to the way they are so important to us.

The dog occupies a significant place in our daily lives. As a companion and co-worker, the dog has been an our side since before the dawn of civilization. Their loyalty to humans over the centuries is legendary, and this loyalty has been reciprocated for the most part, forming a relationship that is unmatched between us and any other members of the animal kingdom.

This book is a celebration of the dog world and our relationship with it. It also celebrates the myriad of breeds, from powerful German Shepherds and Rottweilers to hard-working retrievers and Collies; from life-saving Bloodhounds and St Bernards to breeds such as Lhasa Apsos and Toy Poodles that are bred especially for their aesthetic appeal.

Training and love have made the dog a perfect companion to humans. The indefinable bond that exists between dog and person is mirrored in the dog's eyes The dog's popularity is based on something more than mere utility, for other domestic animals of far greater economic importance are never

Below: A little mixed-breed pup with apparent Poodle heritage.
Opposite: Originally bred in Switzerland, the Bernese Mountain Dog is a beautiful, well-proportioned animal.

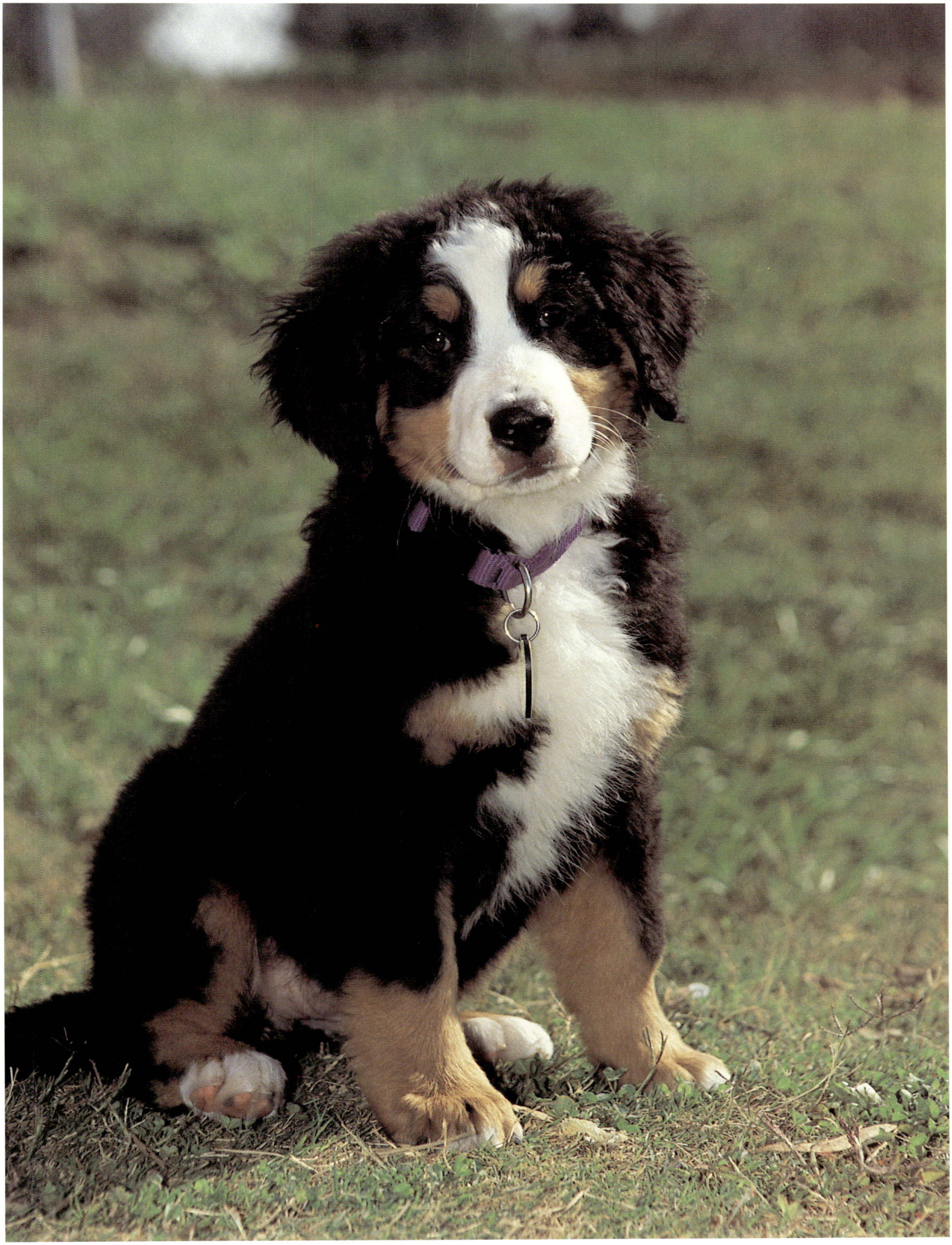

Below: This Golden Retriever is ready for action. Most dogs thrive on exercise and love to run and play.
Right: A little mixed-breed terrier.
Opposite: As this puppy clearly demonstrates, pets are often an excellent form of therapy for humans of any age. If well treated, this pup will grow into a loyal companion.

thought of in the same way as the dog. To most of us, the dog appeals directly to our better nature. Once a dog was regarded as property, but today it is a companion. The dog has greatly benefited by its association with humans and vice versa.

The great French naturalist Georges Leopold Cuvier wrote fervently that the dog represents the most important conquest ever made by humankind. Call it conquest, partnership, association, or whatever, it is only because of the dog's loyalty that any such relationship is possible. The fact that the dog considers its owner above itself illustrates its faculty for complete submergence of personality. This, on many occasions, has enabled it to cope with the egotism of mankind. The dog has an almost universal appeal to members of the human family, regardless of geographical location, age, and position on the social scale. It fits into the hovel as well as the mansion and asks for only one thing — human companionship. The normal dog gives its affection and loyalty unstintingly and recognizes its owner as the center of its universe.

The dog is a beautiful creature, lithe and fluid in motion. The dog is also a creature of great intelligence, tempered by instincts bred over millions of years. Before any real thought had been given to the subject of the canine mind, the animal was chiefly considered to be a creature of reflexes and instincts, with the latter being an accumulation of the former. The blinking of the eyelids at the approach of any foreign object to the eye is an example of a reflex act. A reflex act, therefore, is readily understandable, so we will move on to instincts. There are many aspects to this phenomenon.

As GJ Romanes wrote, 'Instinct is a generic term comprising all those faculties of mind which lead to the conscious performance of actions that are adaptive in character but pursued without necessary knowledge of the relation between the means employed and the ends obtained.' Therefore, although both are hereditary, an instinctive act differs from a reflex act mainly because it is accompanied by consciousness.

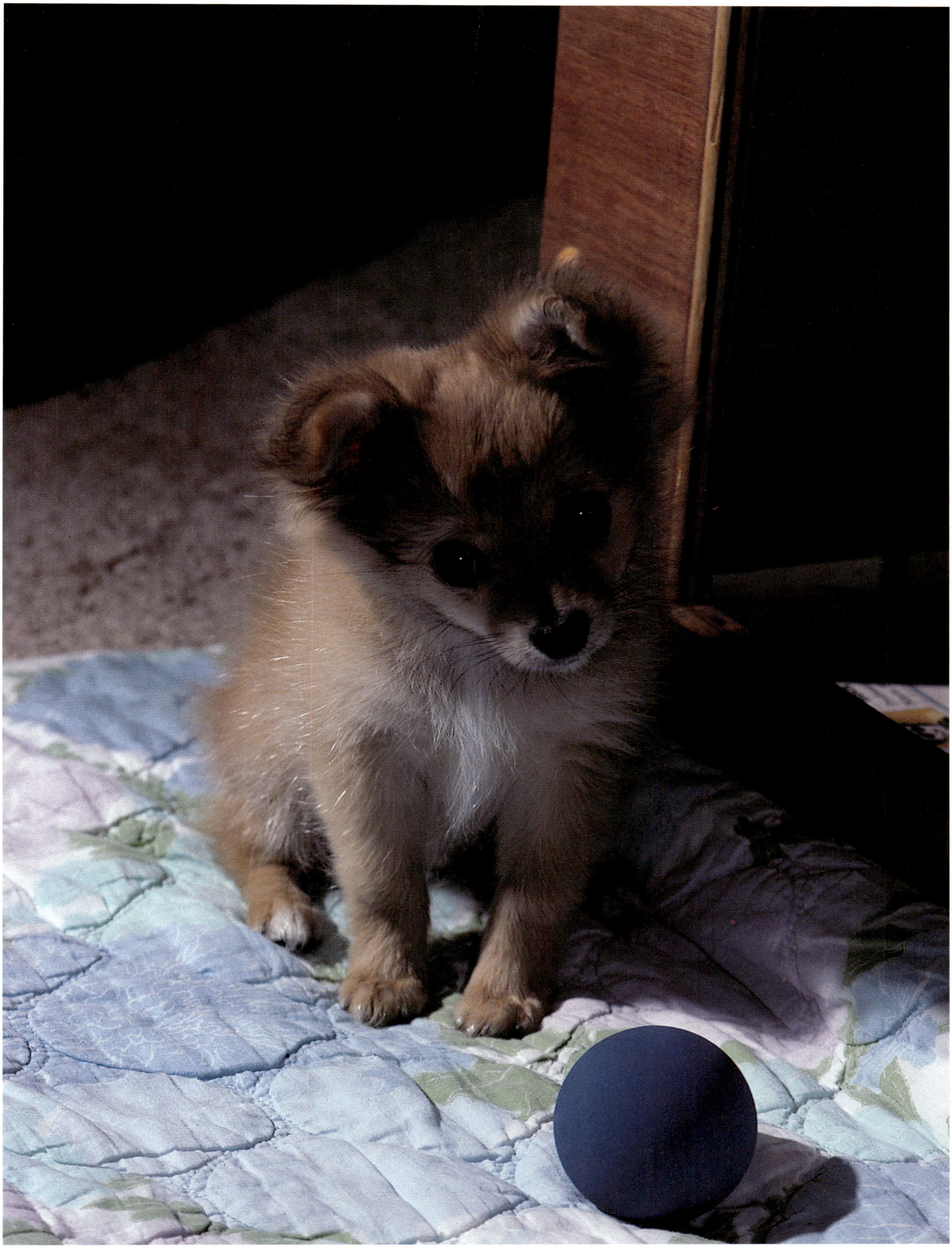

Below: While still bred as guard dogs, Rottweilers also make excellent and reliable pets.
Opposite: The alert face of a Collie-Shepherd mix.

The dog is acknowledged throughout the world. In its unassuming manner, the dog is responsible for saving countless human lives. Dogs are also bred for duty in guiding the blind, a true and thorough testament to canine intelligence and loyalty. As a result of the protective instinct being a part of the dog's very fiber, we are constantly aware of instances of dogs saving human lives. One has only to watch a dog who has been given the custody of a child, especially one just able to get about, to see how alert and fussy about its charge a dog can be — and how sensitive to every danger and prepared to prevent trouble it is. Certain breeds are better for this purpose than others, and while we associate the protection and preservation of human life with members of the larger breeds, it is an instinct common to all dogs.

Then too, the dog naturally assumes the role of the protector of the premises. The trait is common to all breeds, and may be considered a part of the guardian instinct. The smallest dog resents intrusion into its owner's domain to the same degree as its larger brother. What the dog may lack in size is more than compensated for by the determination with which it asserts itself. As a matter of fact, some smaller breeds are preferred for this duty. Naturally, a great deal depends on the temperament of the individual as well as that of the dog. Larger dogs are obviously the more impressive guardians, frequently accomplishing more by virtue of their size than by any individual inclination. The owner of a puppy is often surprised at how early an age this trait becomes evident. On reflection, this is not an unusual condition, however, for we may consider that this useful quality has existed since before the Neolithic era and has continued on through the ages.

The dog's intelligence has been described as responsible for its adaptability to any environment, harsh or kind. The happiness displayed by canines transcends any reasoning

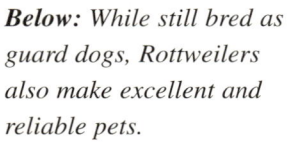

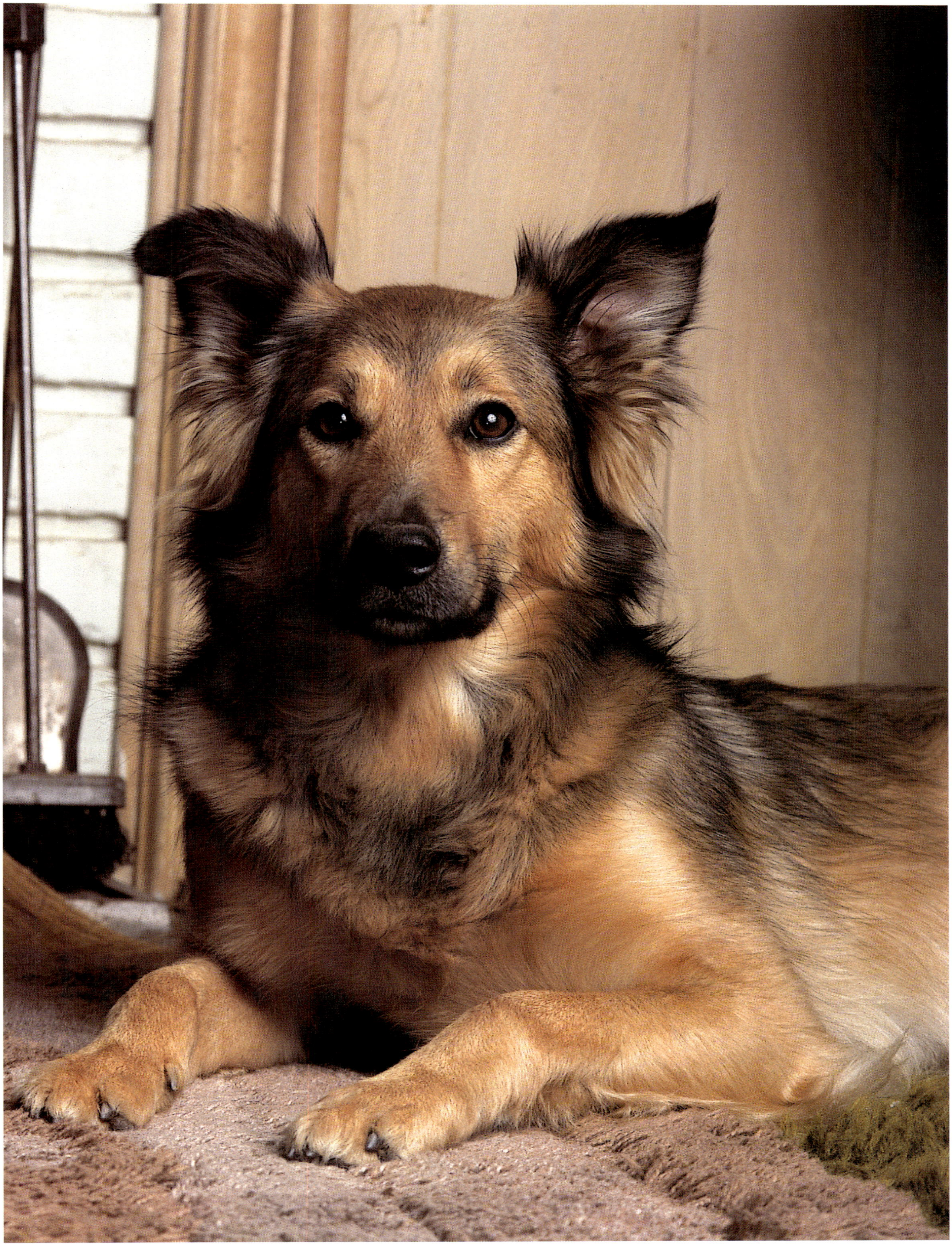

Below: This Bearded Collie is clearly demonstrates the maxim that a dog is indeed 'man's best friend.'
Opposite: This little Jack Russell Terrier pup is obviously having a good time.

and is one of blind devotion. The dog's mind is very receptive, and this may explain many incidents where a dog seems to have a premonition of impending tragedy or other events. 'Sensitivity' is another way of referring to this quality. The dog which has been reared in an atmosphere of emotional instability will absorb enough of the surrounding tension to acquire a distinctly nervous temperament. The dog that gives its distressed owner comfort seems to be reading his thoughts. We have lots of additional evidence for this empathic quality.

Training and love have their points, but most important is the mutual understanding that leads to a complete harmony between the dog and its owner. If the dog is considered as an intelligent animal and not merely a creature of reflexes and instincts, an indefinable bond will come to exist between dog and person, one that has been the subject of countless essays and stories. While it baffles description, it is there. Pet owners may see the relationship as the poet, artist, and writer may attempt to portray it. They are aware of the pleasures derived from daily contact and the poignant sorrow felt after such a pet passes on.

Since the beginning of history, the relationship between a dog and its owner has been nearly perfect. Today, the dog is an integral part of both our daily lives and life styles.

Our dogs are dependable companions and indeed friends. Their popularity, once based on usefulness, is based on something more, a true mutual love, respect and comradeship. Indeed, the dog is really 'man's best friend.'

13

THE ORIGIN OF THE DOG

Below: The Pembroke Welsh Corgi was first bred to herd cattle.
Opposite: With similar dogs having been portrayed in ancient Egyptian temple paintings, the Basenji is recognized as one of the earliest known breeds.

The origin of the dog has always been a subject of interest. The dog is the oldest of the domesticated animals, with Lower Oligocene fossil remains of *canidae*, members of the dog family, having been found in North America. The earliest precursors of *Canis familiaris*, today's dog, are estimated to date back 40 million years. The canine family is composed of two branches: (1) *Cynodictis*: the progenitor of the present day dogs, wolves, foxes, other wild dogs, and members of the raccoon family as well; and (2) *Daphoenus*: the common parent of both giant dogs and bears. The *Cynodictis gregarius* possibly may have been the great-grandfather of the dog family and most likely had a similar form to today's wolfhound.

Cynodictis of this period and the later Eocene probably preyed upon purely herbivorous animals. The intermediate steps in the evolution of the prehistoric *Cynodictis* into the various types of wolves, foxes, and dogs will, no doubt, be linked together as the finding and assembling of fossils continues. The finding of an isolated fossil such as *Cynodictis* is extremely important in formulating theories about the beginning and descent of the dog family. To possess a real significance, however, these skeletons must be found in conjunction with human remains; to have a definite appeal, a true study of the dog must be based upon its relationship with mankind.

Charles Darwin concluded that 'The domestic dogs of the world are descended from two well-defined species of wolf (*Canis lupus* and *Canis latrans*) and from two or three other doubtful species (namely, the European, Indian, and North African wolves); from at least one or two South American ca-

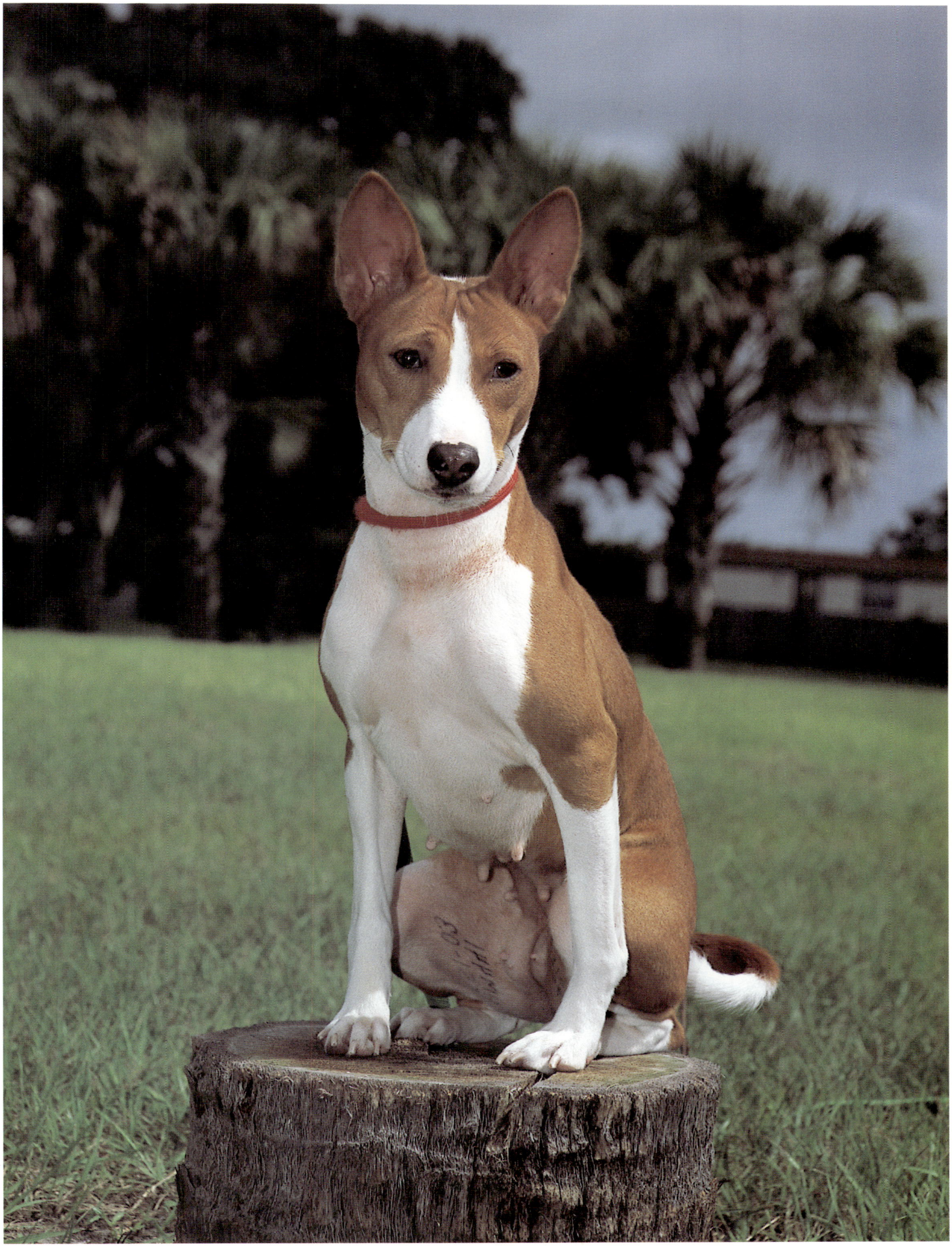

Below: The stately Afghan hound.
Opposite: The Norwegian Elkhound is one of northern Europe's oldest breeds.

nine species; from several races or species of jackal; and perhaps from one or more other extinct species.'

The transition from the wild dog of the Eocene, who preyed on anything edible, to the helper of the Neolithic person, was a slow process. Early relations between wild dog and humans were not friendly. Eventually, however, a basis of understanding developed, and people began to make dogs part of their communities. They utilized the wild dog's power of scent and its ability to procure food for their own purposes.

Humans reasoned that they would benefit by associating with the wild dog. By doing so, they would remove at least one enemy from their list and gain a hunting ally and protector as well. This era, the beginning of humankind's friendship with the dog, was thus a powerful force in the advancement of civilization. The period of time necessary to consummate such an understanding was, no doubt, great, and we can imagine that it was accomplished by following the path of least resistance. This would naturally involve finding wild dog puppies and rearing them in caves. When grown, these would be less wild than their parents; succeeding offspring would be still more amenable to such a relationship with humans.

It is difficult to fix any definite time for the beginning of a more or less continuous association, but an approximate period would be the Neolithic or Stone Age. Enough data has been collected to indicate that by 10,000 BC, humans used dogs to solve some of their problems of existence. The people of the Neolithic age were probably often accompanied by the dog. Discoveries made in the kitchen middens along the coasts of Denmark and Scotland give evidence of a Neolithic community in which the dog was the only domesticated animal. The remains

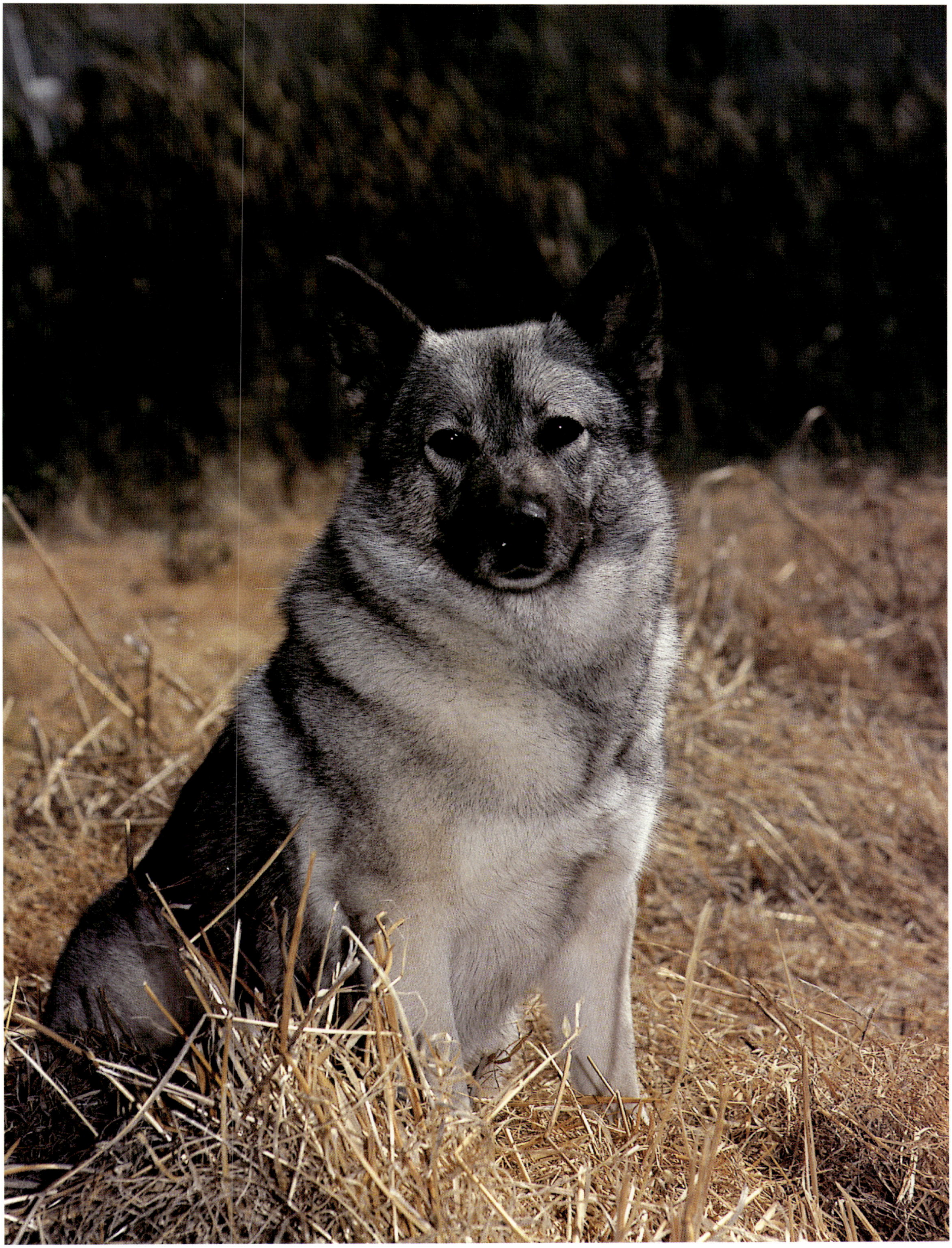

Below: The Pomeranian is a lively little dog that is probably descended from a larger breed such as the Samoyed.
Opposite: The determined face of a Saluki puppy. As he grows, he will develop the long snout and slender neck that characterize of the breed. Salukis were bred in Sumeria 7000 years ago.

of lake dwellers in Switzerland from about 5000 BC indicate a similar association between dog and human.

Gradually, a mutual trust and affection developed. Darwin has pointed out that natural instincts are lost under domestication, while new ones are acquired. We may assume that during this period, the animal's instinctive wariness of humans was slowly replaced by a feeling of love. A gradual metamorphosis took place in the dog's reaction to its new mode of living, and by the advent of the later Neolithic age, dogs could be depended upon for other things besides hunting for food. Its talents were diverted into other channels, for example, protecting sheep, cattle and goats from depredations and guarding the home as well as its occupants. At this time, there was no particular need for a specialized form, but dogs had already undergone some variation in conformation and characteristics. Any early departures from the common ancestor's form were probably not deliberate, but represented natural variations under domestication. Since this occurred independently in several parts of the world, the dog's form in any given region was modified by the climate and terrain of the country where the animal existed. In support of this theory, we have the fossilized remains of the *Canis palustris* of the Neolithic period, whose form suggests that this is the ancestor of the Spitz, Samoyed and some Terriers. The fossils from this era in other parts of the world will give us a better picture of other breeds' progenitors.

As the problems of an evolving human culture became more complex, people often found it necessary, for practical purposes, to alter the conformation of their dogs. The animal thus progressed from the stage of unconscious variation to one of deliberate change. The resulting modifications in form and characteristics depended to a great degree on the resourcefulness of the breeder. As humans improved, corresponding changes affected dogs. Variations produced in the early years never passed the stage of

19

Below: Siberian Huskies have been used by the people of the far north for centuries, and still serve as sled dogs.
Opposite top: A long-coated Chihuahua.
Opposite bottom: A St Bernard takes a well-deserved nap. They are named for the seventeenth century Hospice of St Bernard at Menthon in Switzerland, whose monks used the big dogs to help rescue travellers lost in the Alps.

pure necessity, for humans, as yet, were interested in the dog only as an aid in hunting and protection. Just how much the dog was then valued as a companion is unknown, but people required more leisure than they then had to appreciate this quality of the dog to the fullest extent. When that stage in human culture was reached, the basis was laid for the development of new breeds. The establishment of the social order would, for instance, create a demand for toy breeds, whose sole purpose for being developed was to provide an outlet from the sheer boredom of an inactive life.

There is no doubt that the early breeds bore a strong resemblance to some present breeds. The primary direct proof of this is found in the tracings on the walls of caves and the carvings of the Assyrian and Egyptian civilizations.

A tablet in the British Museum, taken from the ruins of Nineveh, depicts an Assyrian hunting scene from 2,500 years ago. The dogs in it resemble the Mastiff and Great Dane of today. Ancient Egyptian paintings show dogs of the greyhound type, such as the Saluki. It may be one of the oldest pure breeds, having been used in ancient Persia for hunting gazelle.

There is evidence that wherever humans wandered, their dogs accompanied them. After dogs were domesticated by humans throughout Europe, Africa and Asia, they accompanied humans on the great migration across the Bering Land Bridge to North America, and eventually on to South America. Despite the similar relationship between dogs and humans throughout the world, there is an amazing spectrum of differences between dog breeds. As a result, we have animals whose breeds are scattered all over the world and have adapted themselves perfectly to every environment. For example, the Mexican Chihuahua weighs one pound and the St Bernard weighs almost 200 pounds. The size differences suggest that these two breeds could not possibly have come from a common ancestor, and certainly not one resembling a wolf. However, this all starts to make sense when one considers the variations that have taken place over thousands of years: different climactic conditions, the crossing of several different strains, and most importantly, the artificial selection of breeding stock by humans. The latter is particularly true of the last 200 years, in which the principles of breeding have been established and many new breeds developed. In the process of evolution, under the pressure of the above regulating factors, it is only nat-

ural that many of the original parent forms would have been obliterated.

The dog was also important in the mythology of early humans. In ancient Egypt, the dog was a symbol of divinity, with its figure appearing on temple decorations. According to Herodotus, when a dog died the members of the family shaved — an expression of mourning. Their feeling for the dog had a logical basis, for they believed that the appearance of the dog star Sirius was responsible for the overflowing of the Nile, with its resultant fertilizing effect on the inundated lands.

The Greek philosopher Xenophon described two types of Spartan dogs, and there is also a reference to a memorial tablet to a dog being erected at Marathon. Folklore abounds with references, and each nation has its own reasons for commending their respective dogs. St Eustace was regarded as the patron of dogs in southern Europe and St Hubert, for dogs in northern Europe. Indeed, the dog has occupied an important place in human lives throughout history.

Today, the dog's place in human culture is firmly established, with the dog playing an important part in our daily lives. We have come to depend our dogs for many things, material and otherwise. The dog's popularity is indeed based on something more than mere utility, as our dog appeals to something deeper.

Below: An American Eskimo Dog puppy. The United Kennel Club recognizes this dog as a distinct breed from the similar Malamute and Husky. *Opposite:* The Belgian Tervuren is a fine example of a recently-developed herding breed.

23

CHOOSING A DOG

Below: Mixed breed dogs often make wonderful and loyal companions.
Opposite: Most dogs enjoy the company of people, even if it means this little Shetland Sheepdog must spend time in his master's home office.

The beauty of dogs is enhanced by the fact of their variety. Indeed, a fascinating feature about the study of dogs is the wide variety of breeds available. The breeds are divided into different groups according to the purpose for which the animals are used. The members of each group have certain characteristics common to their respective class. However, each breed is a distinct unit and deserves detailed consideration.

Every breed has its enthusiastic supporters, active and passive, who attend dog shows and often belong to clubs that further the best interests of the breed. A few breeds, however, have no specialty clubs. The active element keeps its dogs at the highest form by carefully breeding the best individuals. It is this group that is responsible for making improvements in the breed. The passive element is usually content to own one or more of the dogs, looking to the others for actual leadership.

An official standard of points has been adopted by each club and each dog is judged according to this form. The standard, a guide for judges and breeders alike, states what the ideal dog should look like in size, conformation, color and general appearance. The standard of a breed may be revised if necessary. The purpose that a dog was originally bred for is sometimes altered. Under such conditions, certain modifications in conformation are desirable, and the standard is revised to embrace these changes. There are other reasons for changing it, but the ultimate im-

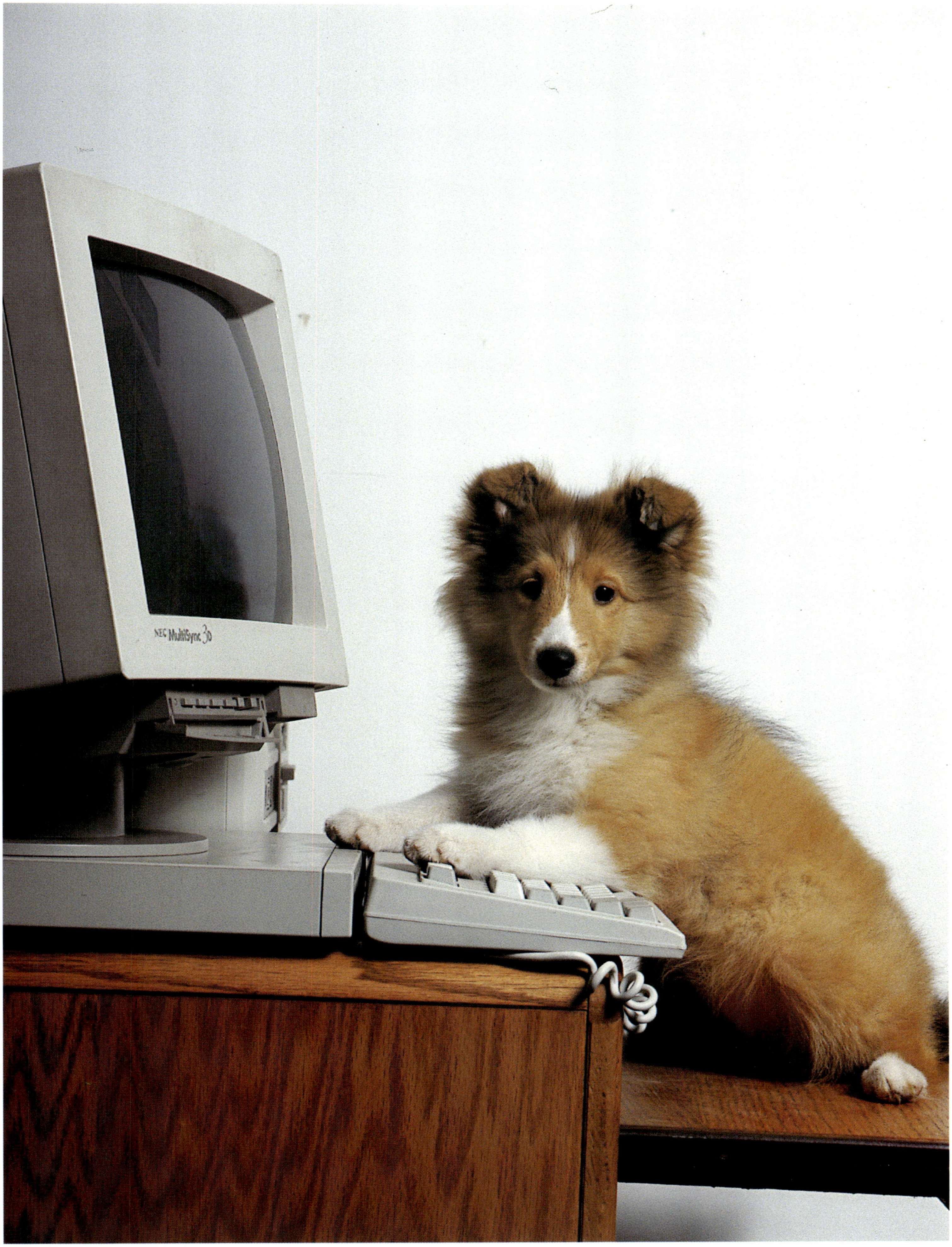
NEC MultiSync 3D

Below: While dogs resembling the Papillon have been found illustrated in manuscripts dating back to the thirteenth century, the breed has only been well established since the nineteenth.
Opposite: Originally bred as a hunting dog, the Beagle makes a wonderful pet, especially for households with children.

provement of the breed is usually the motive. A revised standard does not always meet with unqualified approval. It should be kept in mind that alterations enable a breed to cope with changed conditions.

Consideration of the breed type is important when choosing a dog. One may be unable to deny the roguish tilt of a certain terrier's head, while another may feel a tug at their heart occasioned by some hound's forlorn facial expression. It may be a sentimentally sound idea to choose a dog because of a sudden impulse, but this should be discouraged for practical reasons. The dog you take into your home will shortly win its way into your affections and, if it is a puppy, you look forward to years of companionship.

One must have a sense of what one wants in a dog. One should first decide whether a dog is to be a purebred or a mixed breed. If a purebred is chosen, the breed should be suited to its particular purpose. Locale is important. Certain dogs are suitable to be kept in the city, while others need the open space of the country. Other considerations may be the kind of coat, the best age and whether it should be male or female. One should also consider whether the dog will be a family dog — the companion of children and adults — or will give all its time to one person.

In choosing a breed, one has every reason to be particular about this new member of the family. A dog will occupy the home and thoughts, and a great deal of the satisfaction

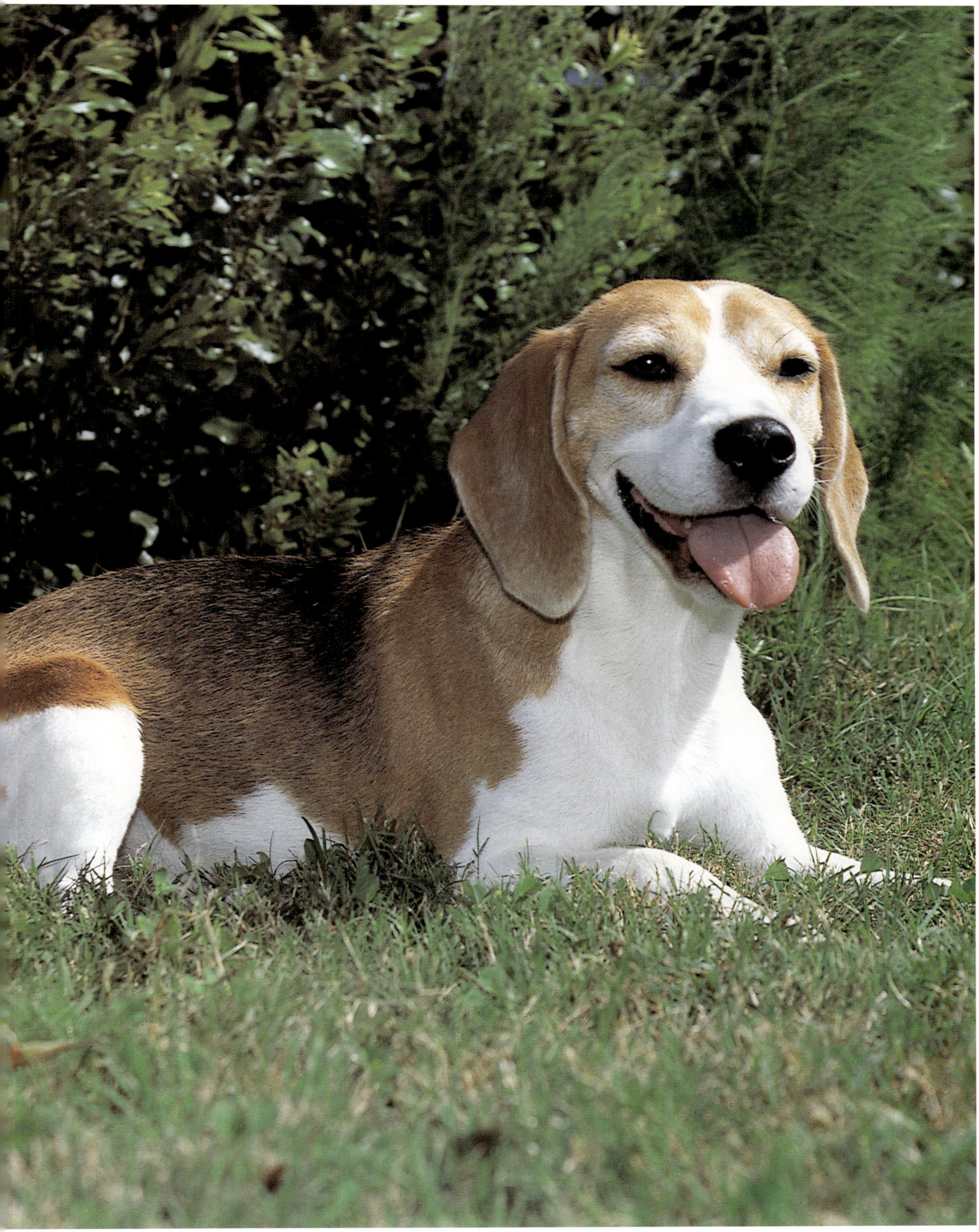

Below: A perky little mixed breed puppy with apparent terrier ancestry.
Opposite: The answer to any young child's dreams, this little puppy resembles his Yorkshire Terrier mother in coloration and markings.

experienced by both dog and person will depend on how these questions are decided.

Purebred versus mixed breed dog is a question which has been argued by dog lovers for many years and will probably never be decided to the complete satisfaction of all parties. Opinions vary from a positive preference for one or the other to a lukewarm stand bordering on indifference. An unqualified stand either way merely expresses the individual's preference. While many feel that the purebred represents the logical choice, both sides of the question should be discussed. The buyer will, in any event, follow his own inclination. In the case of a dog used exclusively as a house pet and companion, the choice is optional.

However, if the dog is to be used for any specialized purpose, there can be no compromise — it must be an appropriate breed. For example, a German Shepherd can be trained to retrieve but a Labrador Retriever is born and bred for such tasks.

Many people do prefer the purebred. Its ancestry is known and it will conform to the traits of its breed. Most owners also take a real pride in the pedigree and appearance of their pet, and enjoy hearing flattering remarks about both. The person who strives for perfection in all things is naturally inter-

29

Below: Barely weaned, this little pup will soon be ready for a good home.
Opposite top: A lop-eared, long-haired terrier pup.
Opposite bottom: A pair of young rascals, the son and daughter of an Australian Kelpie.

ested in the purebred because its conformation is fixed by a standard for that breed. To many, the possession of a smartly turned out, pedigreed dog is not without a certain tonic effect and reassurance. A well-bred dog at the end of a leash does, in great measure, reflect upon the well-dressed person exercising it.

Those who love mixed breed dogs will argue that many of the above points refer to superficialities and the psychological effect on the owner, rather than having any bearing on the dog's intrinsic worth. This, in a sense, is true. The term 'mutt' does not imply anything hideous. At worst, the mixed breed's appearance is only nondescript, but its charm is often so great that we completely lose sight of its exterior. The oddest-looking mutt is not without a certain dignity of manner. The mixed breed dog has given satisfaction in many homes and its pet status is universally acknowledged. The love and devotion a dog is capable of showing is, after all, independent of pedigree. The price of the mixed breed dog is not always a factor. In many cases the love for a mutt may be partly explained by the human desire to help the underdog. A dog of mixed ancestry is often described as having more intelligence and character than the purebred. It has also been asserted that the mixed breed dog is healthier, but there is no real basis for the claim.

The mixed breed dog is the mainstay of both Working Companion Dogs and Dogs for the Deaf. These special dogs, many of whom are often saved from the pound, are trained to be companions and helpers to the deaf. They alert their owners to smoke alarms, telephones, alarm clocks and doorbells. Like guide dogs for the blind, hearing dogs are permitted to accompany their owners into restaurants, stores and other public buildings. Because of dogs, many deaf and blind people can have happy and productive lives.

There are many stories throughout history about the courage and loyalty of mixed breed dogs. As recently as New Year's Eve, 1994, a 'mutt' saved her family's lives. Rosie, a Shepherd and Collie mix, woke Madga Berrios early that morning, insisting that she had to go outside. When Ms Berrios opened the door and the fresh air blew in her face, she realized that she was ill and that something was terribly wrong. Then, 'Everybody started getting up. It looked like we were drunk — dizzy and nauseous.'

The family began opening windows and her husband, Miguel Berrios, called 911. All nine family members were treated for carbon monoxide poisoning and released from the hospital. 'Our Rosie, to us she's a hero. This could have turned into a tragedy.'

For many, however, the purebred, who represents generations of carefully selected breeding strains, is more dependable. It requires no more care and will not eat any more food. For them, the thrill of having a well-bred dog decides the issue.

The dog's age may be considered next and the puppy is by far the best choice. It is true the puppy must be trained in the ways of cleanliness, but this is not the ordeal that the novice imagines. The veterinarian, breeder and local SPCA will have many brochures and suggestions for the new dog owner.

The puppy is most subject to illness during the first ten months of its life. A person wishing to avoid a maximum of bother with such matters will think of the adult dog as the solution to the problem. The adult is generally past the stage of chewing and is properly trained and housebroken. The adult also should have already had all its inoculations. At first glance, it would seem that the mature animal possesses all the advantages, but there are certain disadvantages as well.

To begin with, the puppy has a charm which can be appreciated only if you see one grow up under your care. The activity of the youngster, its irrepressible spirit and mischievousness — all are definitely worthwhile. Watching a puppy develop is more than just a biological affair — it becomes a fascinating study to note the reactions to various situations, and how these reactions change with maturity. Since puppyhood represents the formative period of the dog's life, it is better that you influence the molding of its personality. You will find the puppy absorbing certain qualities from your temperament and the general environment. The puppy's impressions become woven into the strands of its makeup. The degree to which this will happen depends largely on the sensitivity of the dog.

It should be readily seen from the foregoing that a dog reared from puppyhood under your guidance is in every sense your dog, adding much to the satisfaction of ownership. For practical purposes, it is better to get a young dog when there are children in the household. While most older dogs take readily to children in a new home, there have been instances of a strained relationship at the beginning. Mature dogs taken from a kennel or an environment of adults are often bewildered by the antics of children, and thus need a little time to readjust themselves. Children are not always respectful of canine sensibilities, and the growing puppy often learns to accept the playful roughhousing in better spirits than its mature brother.

The very young puppy's cuddly appearance and seeming helplessness is always most appealing. Some experts do not advise getting a dog younger than three months. By this time, the youngster is thoroughly

Below: This little Sheepdog's shaggy, long-haired appearance is what makes the breed so doggone appealing.
Opposite: A cuddly breed, the Chow Chow is often described as being bear-like.

33

weaned and well started on regular food. The dog may have also been wormed by the breeder. Some breeders are now keeping the dogs until they are at least sixteen weeks old so that they may be given their inoculations before being sold.

Usually one of the first points a prospective buyer decides upon is the dog's gender. The average person prefers the male, commonly believing that he is the steadier of the two, and therefore makes a better pet. However, the female is just as desirable and often better than her male counterpart. She is less of a wanderer, usually better with children, more understanding and sympathetic, and just as dependable under working conditions. Many dog lovers insist on getting a female as a pet. There will also always be those who dislike females, and for this reason alone prefer males.

The size, type of coat and breed of dog will depend on the owner's preference, but should actually be determined by the environment. For practical purposes, it would be better to follow this formula: urban residents should limit their choice to small or medium-sized animals, while suburban and country dwellers have a wider choice. This rule is very important to the animal's well-being. Some preferences exceed the bounds of good sense, resulting in dogs like Great Danes being kept in small apartments. Many large dogs kept under such conditions are surprisingly free from visible disease, but without proper attention and exercise, the dog can become uncontrollable.

For obvious reasons, breeds with heavy coats should be kept where the animal will be comfortable, and this excludes the over heated home. As they do in other things, fads and fancies in dogs exist, and the selection of a dog is often based on nothing better than the present popularity of a particular breed. If a dog is selected with its environment in mind, it will be an ideal situation for the health and comfort of the animal, as well as for the best interests of the owner. On the other hand, acquiring a pet is more often regulated by emotions than by logic. Some will continue to buy pets for the same reasons that they always have — because they buy what pleases them.

Most of the known breeds have been accorded official recognition by one or more kennel clubs. They are divided into sporting dogs, hounds, working dogs, terriers, toys, non-sporting dogs and herding dogs. It is an imposing list, and on it one will find an animal having the qualifications to fit any fancy and environment. In this book it is possible to give only the briefest summary of a few of these dogs.

Below: *This Australian Shepherd is obviously in a good mood and ready for a romp.*
Opposite: *A Shetland Sheepdog at play.*

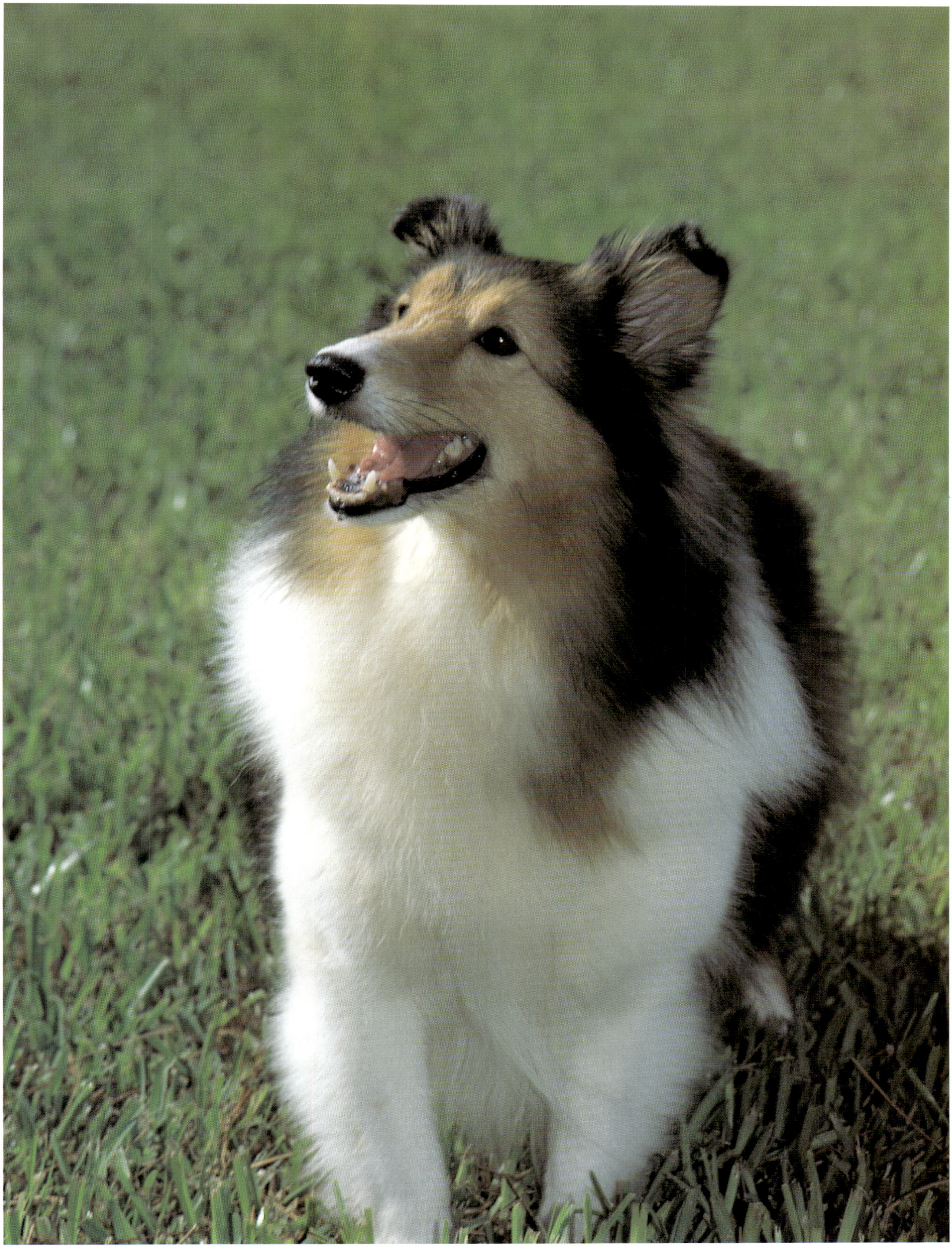

TERRIERS

Below: A scrappy little Norwich Terrier pup.
Opposite: A characteristically alert Jack Russell Terrier.

One of the largest groups of breeds are the terriers. It's members are found throughout the world, belonging to people from every walk of life. This group comprises breeds such as the Airedale, American Staffordshire, Australian, Bedlington, Border, Bull, Cairn, Dandie Dinmont, Fox (Smooth and Wirehaired), Irish, Kerry Blue, Lakeland, Manchester, Miniature Schnauzer, Norfolk, Norwich, Scottish, Sealyham, Skye, Soft Coated Wheaton, Staffordshire Bull, Welsh and West Highland White.

Terriers may be described as medium in size with few exceptions. They have immense courage and a determination to finish a job through, even in the face of death. A terrier is wiry, tough and never backs out of anything. The dogs are lithe and fast, with solid muscle and good bone development. The heads, legs and coat are important structures. The jaws are powerful, with large teeth that facilitate biting and holding the quarry. The legs must be strong with firm feet and tough nails in case it is necessary 'go to earth' or to dig in. In most terriers, the

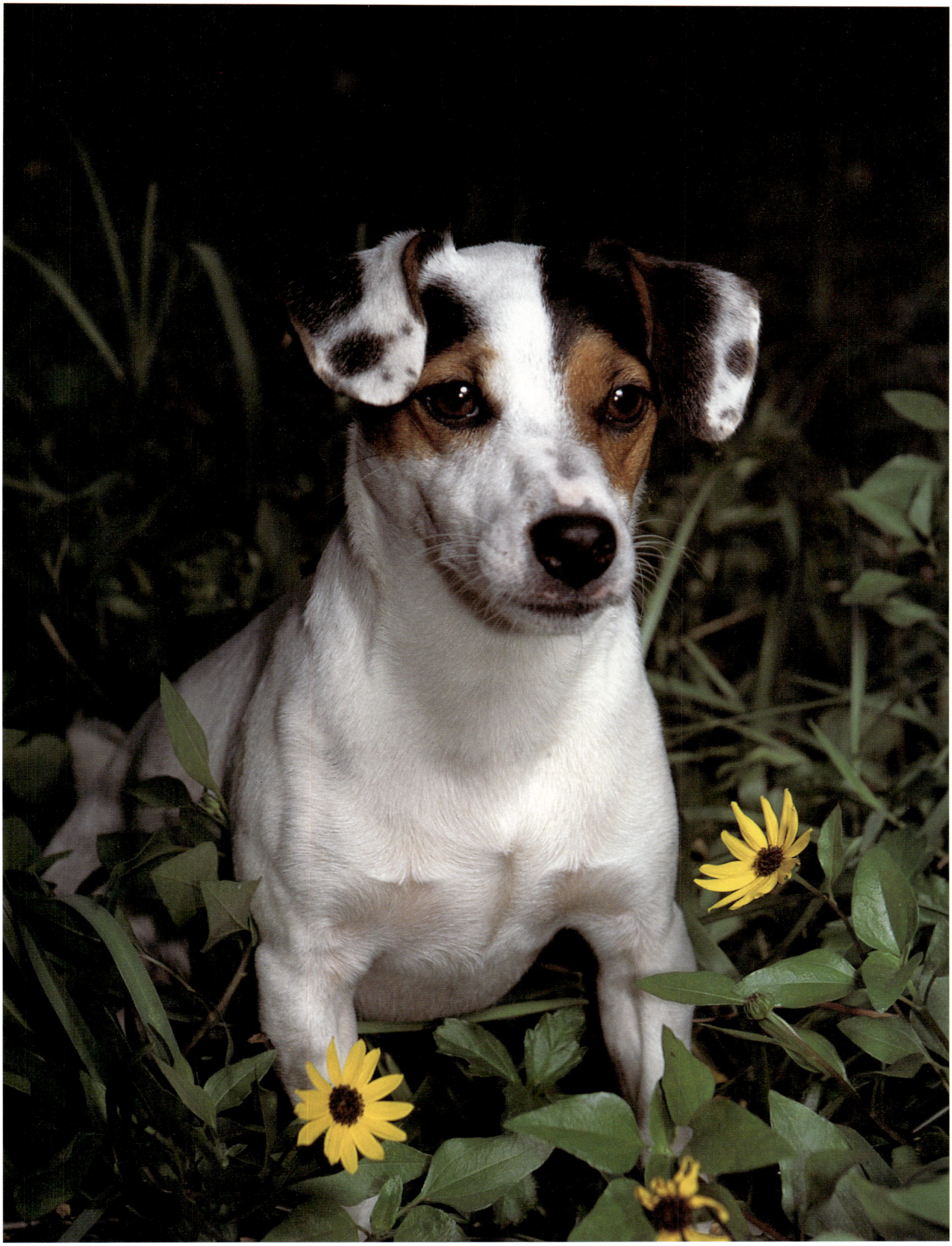

coat is short, close and able to withstand both wear and weather. In addition to all the conformation requirements, this dog must possess the terrier character inherent in the dog's very fiber — spirit and grit. The larger members of the group, such as the Airedale, were once used in the hunting of large game, such as bears.

These dogs make excellent pets and companions. They are suitably sized for small quarters, whether in or out of town, and their engaging personality and lively manner makes them irresistible pets. Many hearing dogs are mixed breed terriers.

The word 'terrier' is derived from the Latin. In 1565, Caius said: 'Of the Dogge called Terrar, in Latine Terrarius. Another sorte of hunting dog there is which hunteth the Foxe and the Badger or Greye only, whom we call Terrars, because they (after the manner and custome of ferrets in searching for Connyes) creepe into the grounds, and by that means make afrayde, nyppe and byte the Fox and the Badger in such sort, that eyther they teare them in pieces with theyr teeth beying in the bosome of the earth or else hayle and pull them perforce out of their lurking angles, dark dungeons, and close caves....'

The meaning is quite clear and proves that the terrier's purpose was established even in those early times. But it was not until the nineteenth century that some of the dogs began to be bred with a specific goal, and the

Below: The Airedale is the largest of all terrier breeds, and a wonderful pet for people that have plenty of room to let them romp.
Opposite: An endearing little terrier mix.

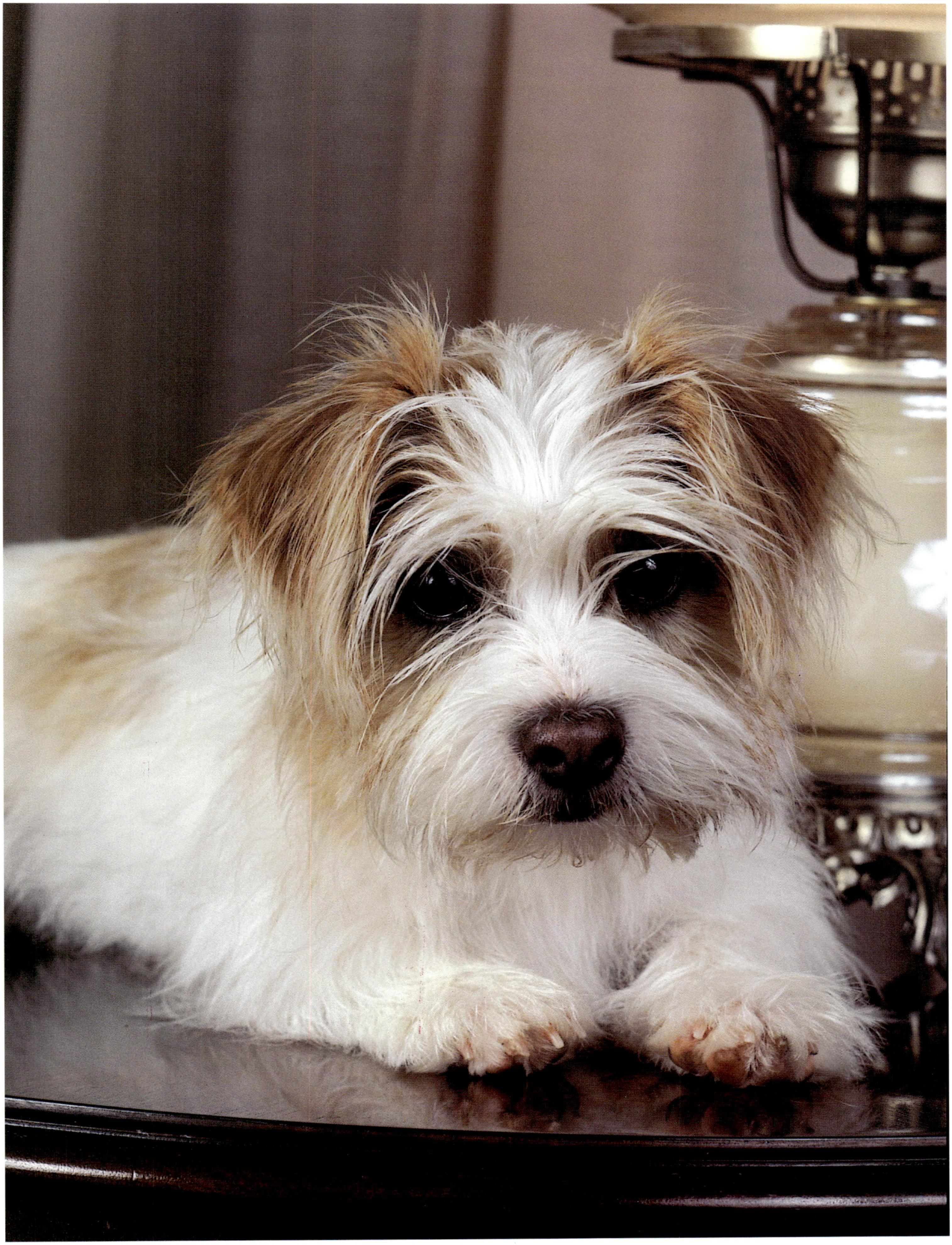

resulting puppies assumed a new importance. It is believed, however, that for many years, before ever being taken outside their original environments, some Scottish terriers were bred for a similar form to their present varieties.

Britain was the place of origin for many of the terrier breeds. Terriers have existed in many parts of the British Isles for hundreds of years, doing the work expected of them. It may have been that the mixed breed hound was the first basis for the terrier strains, and the native English terrier of centuries back may have been a nondescript mutt compared to the modern breeds, but he was the basic stock that the original breeders worked with to build the newer terriers.

Some terriers have docked tails and a few breeds have cropped ears. In conformation,

Below: A little West Highland White Terrier puppy. *Right and opposite:* The Scottish Terrier, known universally as the 'Scottie,' is one of the world's best-loved breeds.

41

the terriers may be regarded roughly according to their place of origin, although certain innate characteristics are common to the entire group.

The Scotch dogs — Cairn, Scotty, Skye and West Highland White — are compact and have fairly short legs. They have strong, weather-resistant coats which one would expect in dogs from that part of the world. It is easy to believe that a common parental stock was responsible for all of them.

The Cairn is a lively little terrier, very intelligent and quite popular. When the casting call went out for *The Wizard of Oz*, director Mervyn LeRoy was looking for a Scottie. '[A] Scottie, a well-educated one, a dog intelligent enough to follow Judy Garland through several sequences of *The Wizard of Oz*.' Instead, trainer Carl Spitz brought over Terry, a female Cairn Terrier. Terry won over the director and cast of the MGM production with her lively personality. She will always be remembered as Dorothy's little dog, Toto.

The Scotty is the debonair and whimsical fellow who has travelled far from its native Highlands. It needs no introduction or description, for Scotties are pictured in all forms of advertising. Their gaiety and charm cannot be denied.

The West Highland White is often called a white Scotty in error. It is a distinct breed, lively and charming enough to receive more recognition than it does. The Skye is a determined, fighting terrier greatly misjudged because of its long, flowing coat.

Below and opposite: Jolly and irresistible, a little West Highland White Terrier. The 'Westie' originated in Argyllshire in Scotland as early as the time of the reign of King James I.

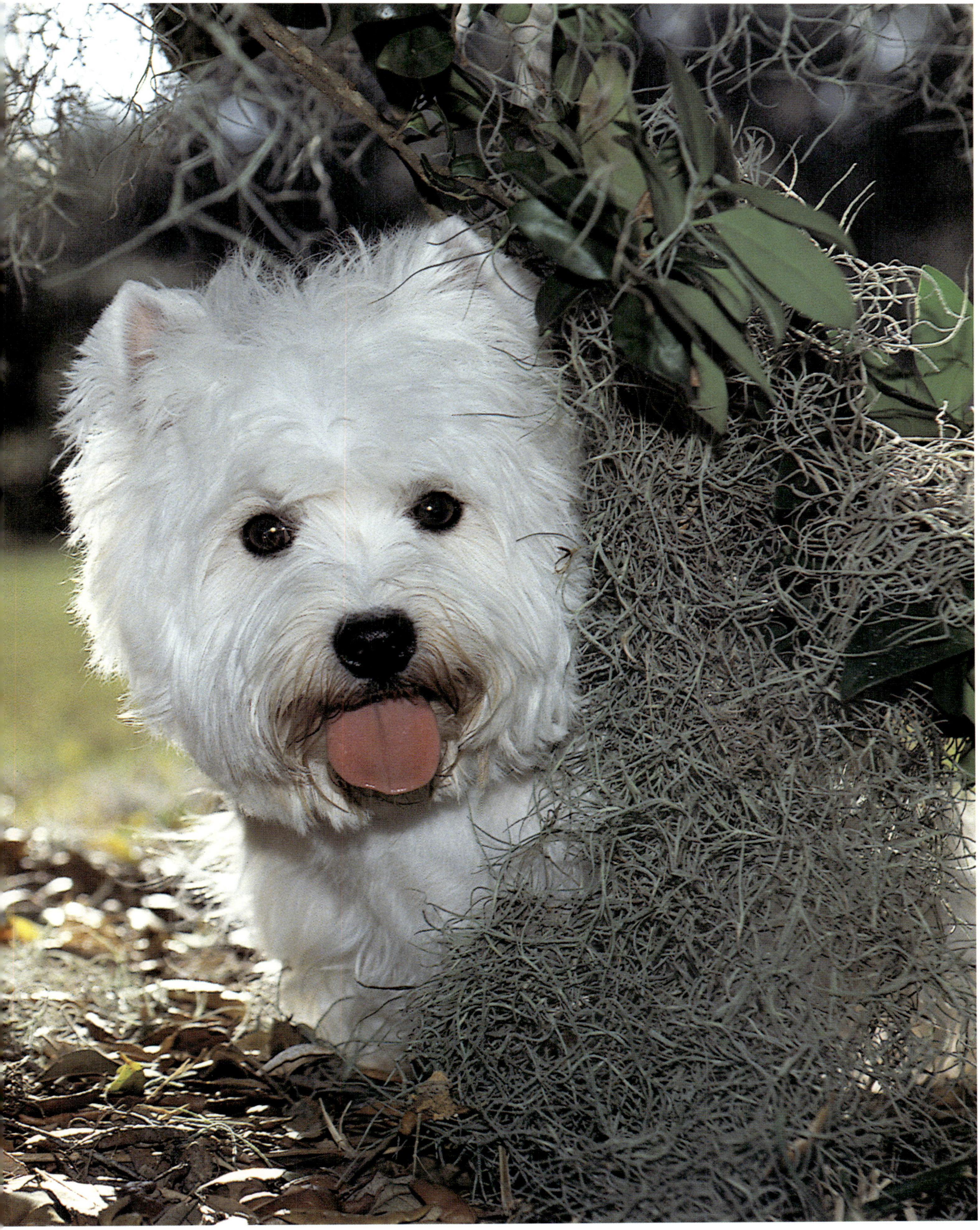

Below: Perking up his ears on call from his master, this Fox Terrier demonstrates the alertness of his breed.
Opposite: Comparing this Border Terrier to the Fox Terrier demonstrates the great variety among terrier breeds.

The terriers of the Border country — Dandie Dinmont, Bedlington and Border — have a growing following in this country. The Dandie and the Bedlington share the honors for being the oddest-looking dogs in the terrier group. The Bedlington is described as having a lamb-like appearance yet it is one of the gamest dogs alive. The Dandie Dinmont, quite low in front and high in the back, is considered an ancestor of the Bedlington. Sir Walter Scott's mention of a Dandie Dinmont is supposed to be responsible for the dog's recognition as a breed. Border Terriers, hardy and spunky, have become popular companion dogs.

The English terriers include the Smooth Fox Terrier, Wirehaired Fox Terrier, Bull Terrier, Airedale, and Manchester Terrier. The Fox Terriers, an old breed, have been well received wherever they've been introduced. They symbolize all the necessary terrier qualities and have stimulated much interest in the terrier group. The Wirehaired Fox is the rough, broken-haired specimen which is otherwise the same as the Smooth. Their temperaments are supposed to be the

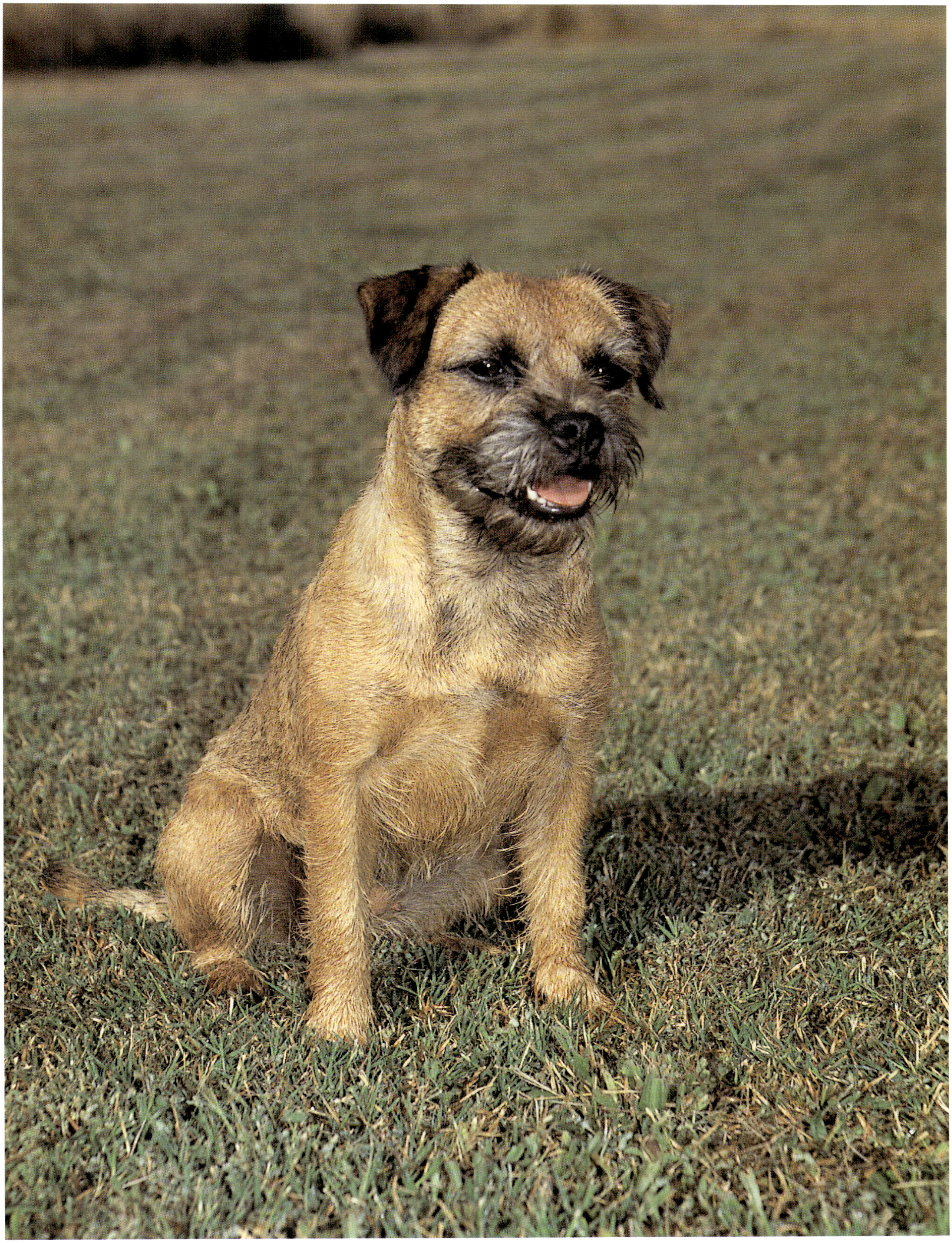

Below: The Bull Terrier is known as the 'White Cavalier.'
Opposite: A happy Airedale poses proudly.

same, but the Wire is believed to have more personality. It is an extremely attractive dog, whose abundance of snap and animation have given it a phenomenal career in the show ring. He is exceedingly popular, and possesses a gaiety that is possibly more spontaneous than the Scotty's, but lacking its philosophical Scotsman manner. The Lakeland Terrier, also from the British Isles, is of average terrier size.

The Airedale is one of the largest of the terriers and the most businesslike. Its compact muscle weighs as much as 45 pounds and the breed is often used as a guard dog, as

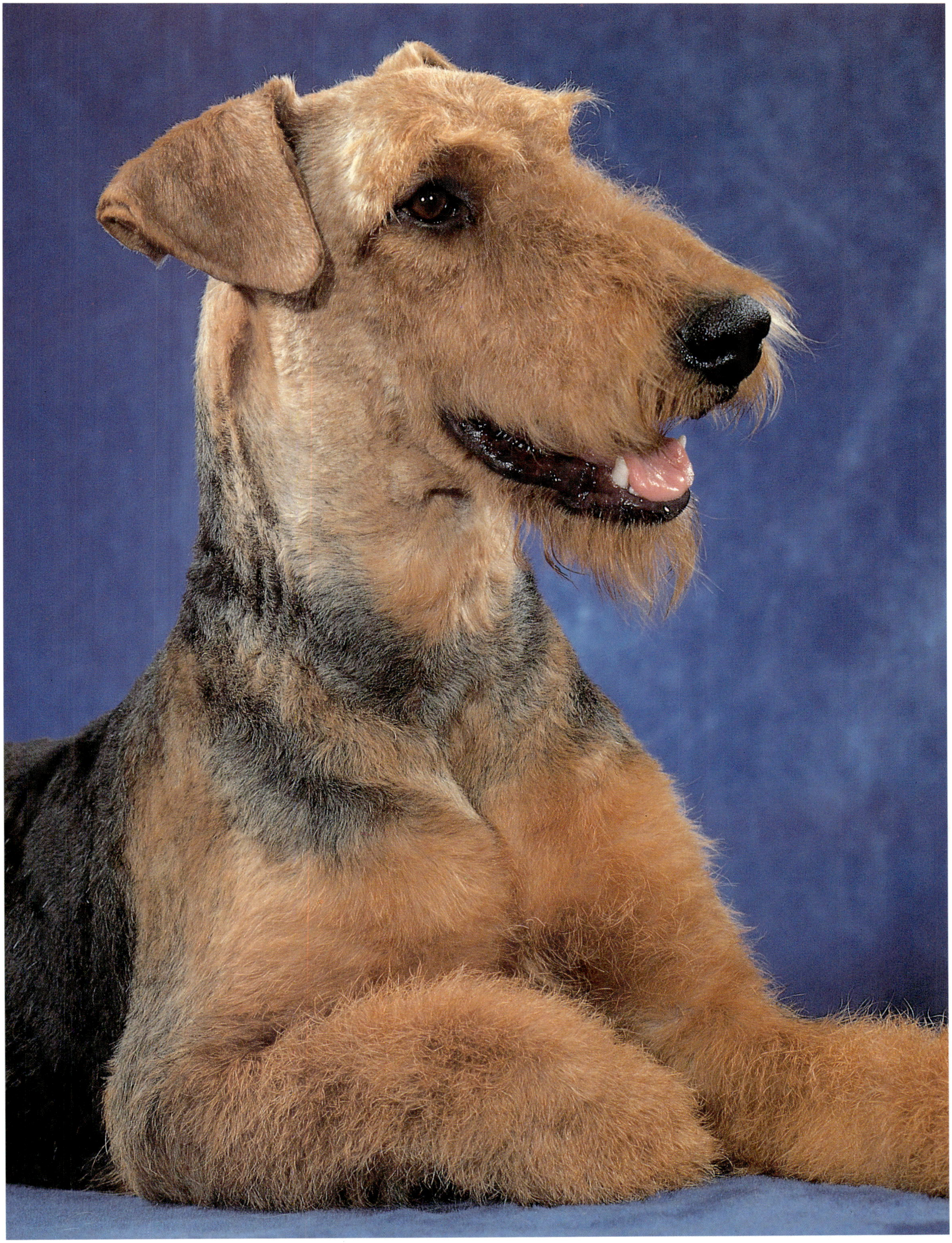

well as for hunting big game in the Rockies and Africa. It is unexcelled as an all-round dog.

The Manchester is the ideal conception of the smooth-coated, clean-looking black-and-tan terrier. The male dog can weigh as much as 22 pounds.

The Bull Terrier, an all-white streak of indomitable courage, is a complete gentleman. The larger Bull Terriers can weigh up to 60 pounds and make excellent guardians. They are no longer used as pit fighting dogs but their old spirit still prevails. They require a firm hand and more loving attention than the other terriers.

The Emerald Isle produced the Irish Terrier, a red-coated bundle of scrappiness and dependable devotion, which makes a fine all-round dog. The Kerry Blue, which is increasing in popularity, comes from the same country and also boasts an unquenchable spirit.

Another of Ireland's traditional terriers is the Soft-Coated Wheaton. Developed as an all purpose farm dog, the Wheaton is a cheerful and devoted companion

Both the Welsh Terrier and the Sealyham originated in Wales. The Welsh Terrier has all the desirable terrier traits and looks like a small Airedale. Sealyhams are compact and hardy little fellows, quite low to the ground, but lack none of the essential terrier characteristics.

Below: The wistful face of a loyal Irish Terrier.
Opposite: A striking pair of Irish Terriers, their coats a beautiful, deep red.
Overleaf: Originally bred in Ireland, the Soft-Coated Wheaton Terrier is an active and energetic breed.

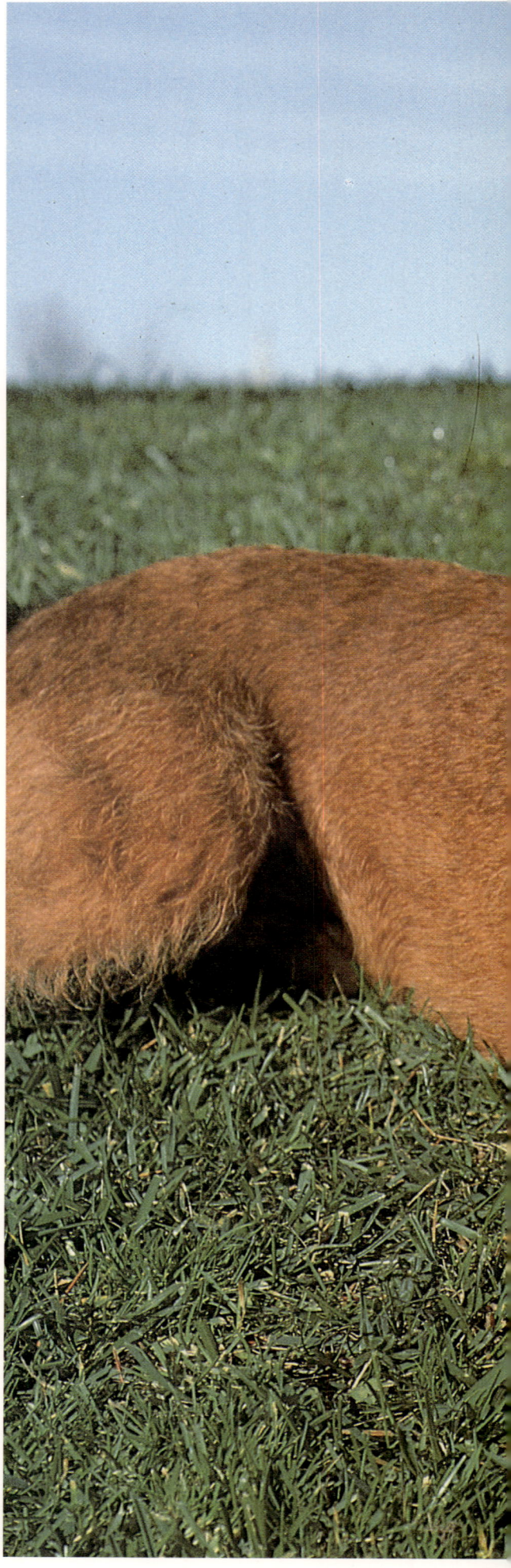

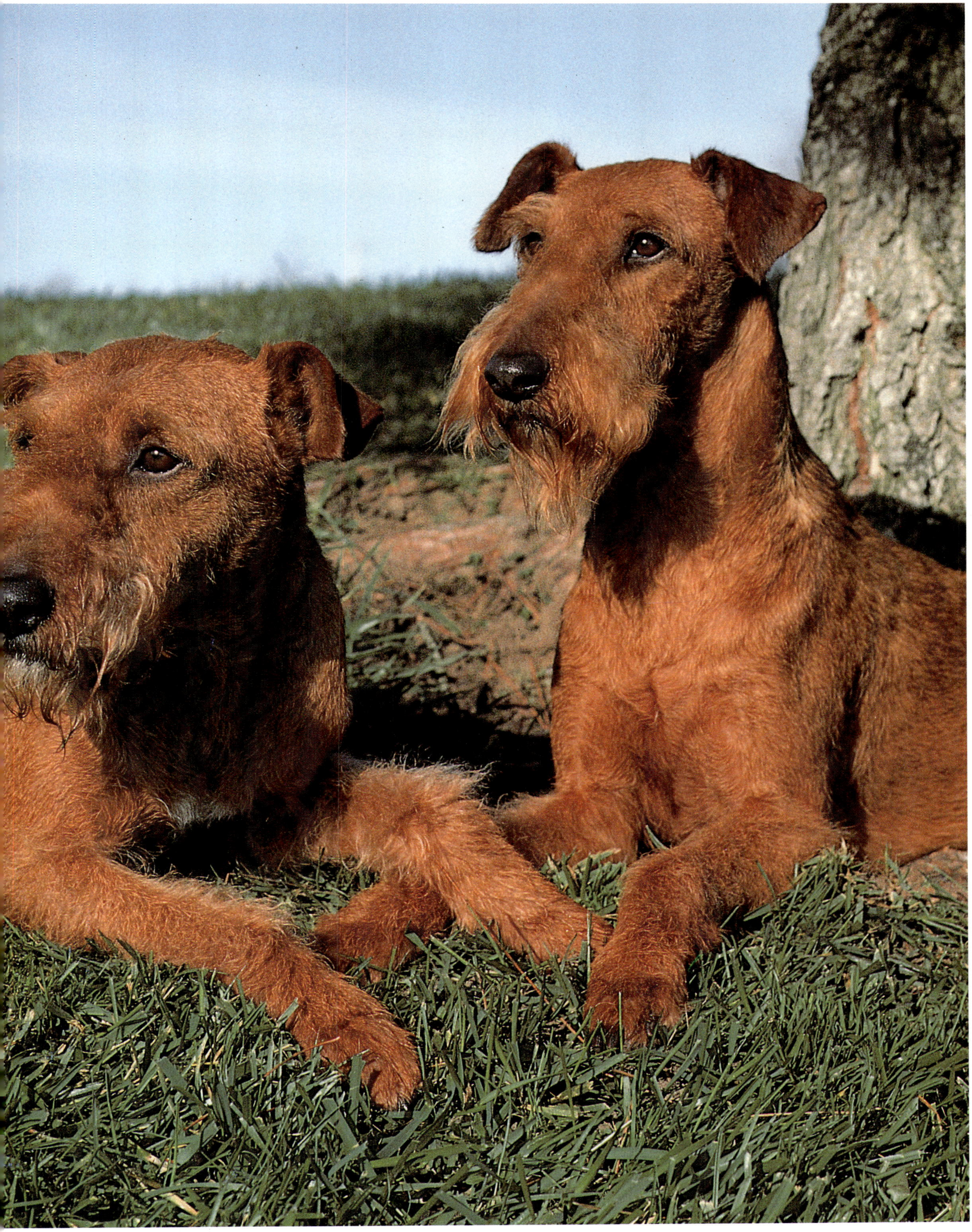

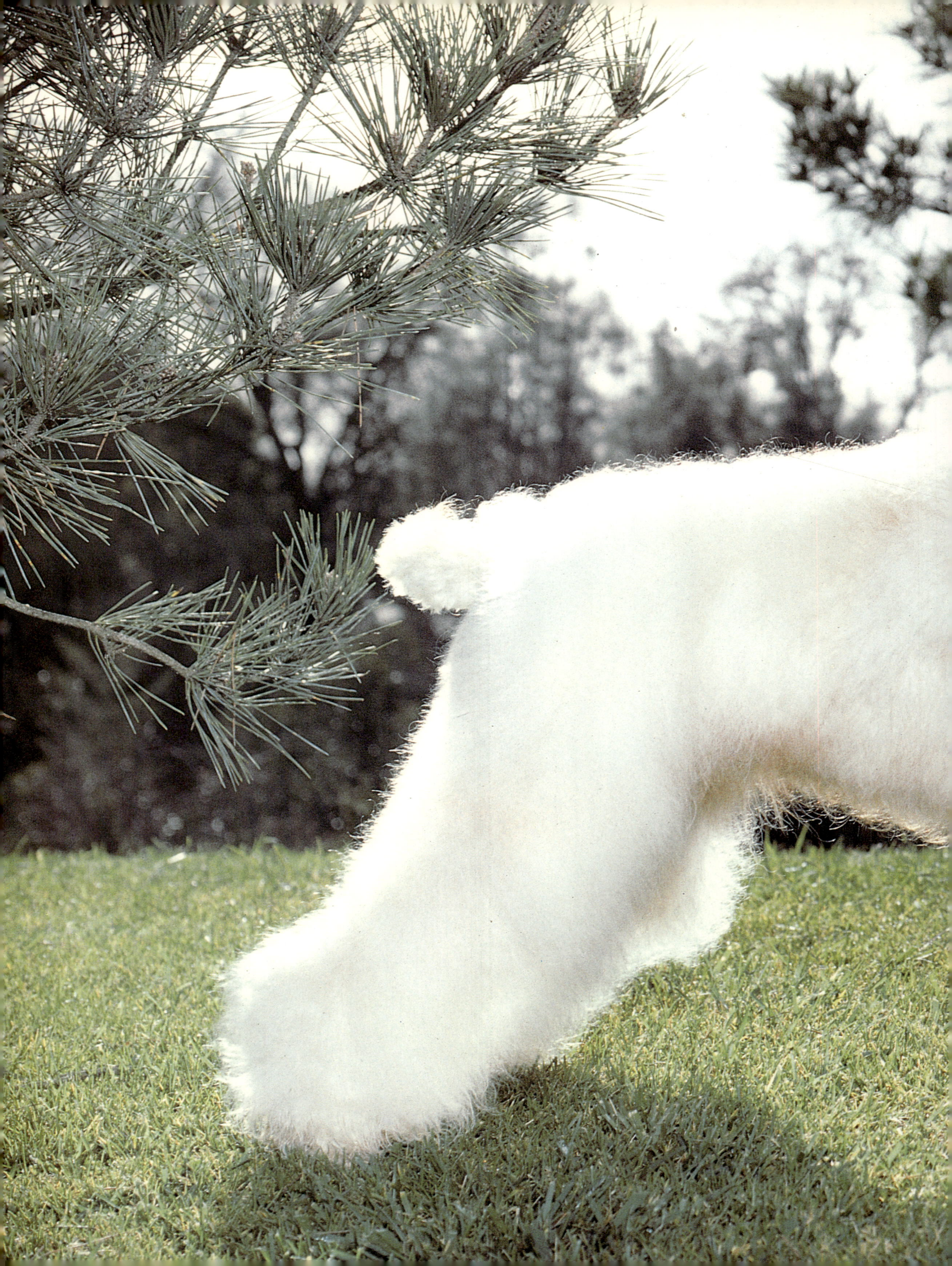

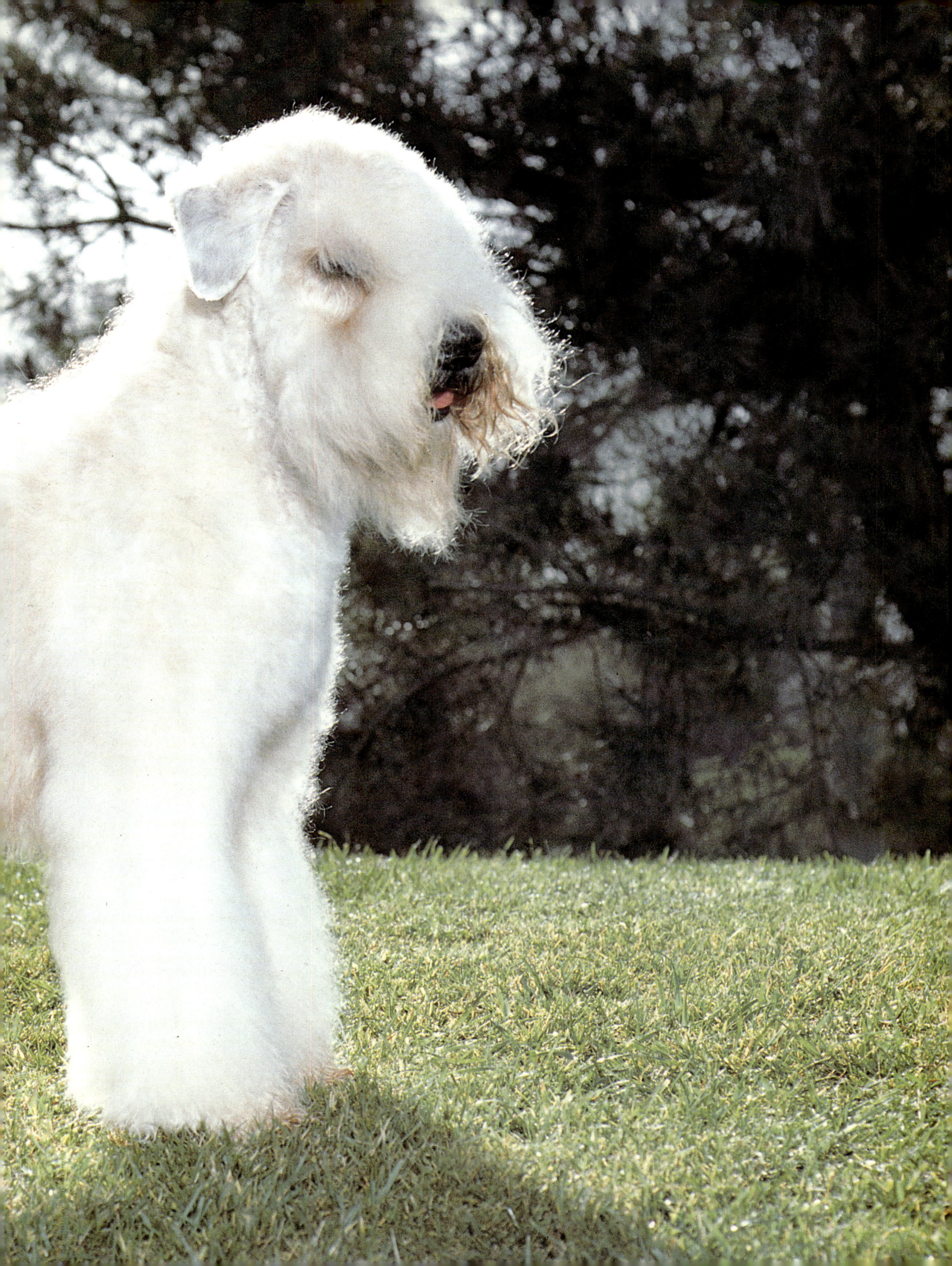

HOUNDS

Below and opposite: Perhaps the oldest of currently existing breeds of dogs, the Afghan Hound is portrayed in a Greek tapestry dating from 500 BC.

Some of the oldest members of the canine family belong to this group, which originated in the Middle East and Southwest Asia at a time when those areas were the crucibles of human civilization. The Saluki, or gazelle hound, came from Persia, which is now Iran, and its conformation today is almost the same as that shown in the earliest available pictures.

Hounds hunt by either sight or scent. The Greyhound, Deerhound and wolfhounds hunt by sight. The Basset, Beagle, Blood, Fox, Harrier, Otter and Elkhounds all locate the quarry by scent. Most hounds kill their prey.

In the hound group are such breeds as the Afghan Hound, Basenji, Basset Hound, Beagle, Black and Tan Coonhound, Bloodhound, Borzois, Dachshund (Smooth, Longhaired and Wirehaired), Scottish Deerhound, American Foxhound, English Foxhound, Greyhound, Harrier, Ibizan Hound, Norwe-

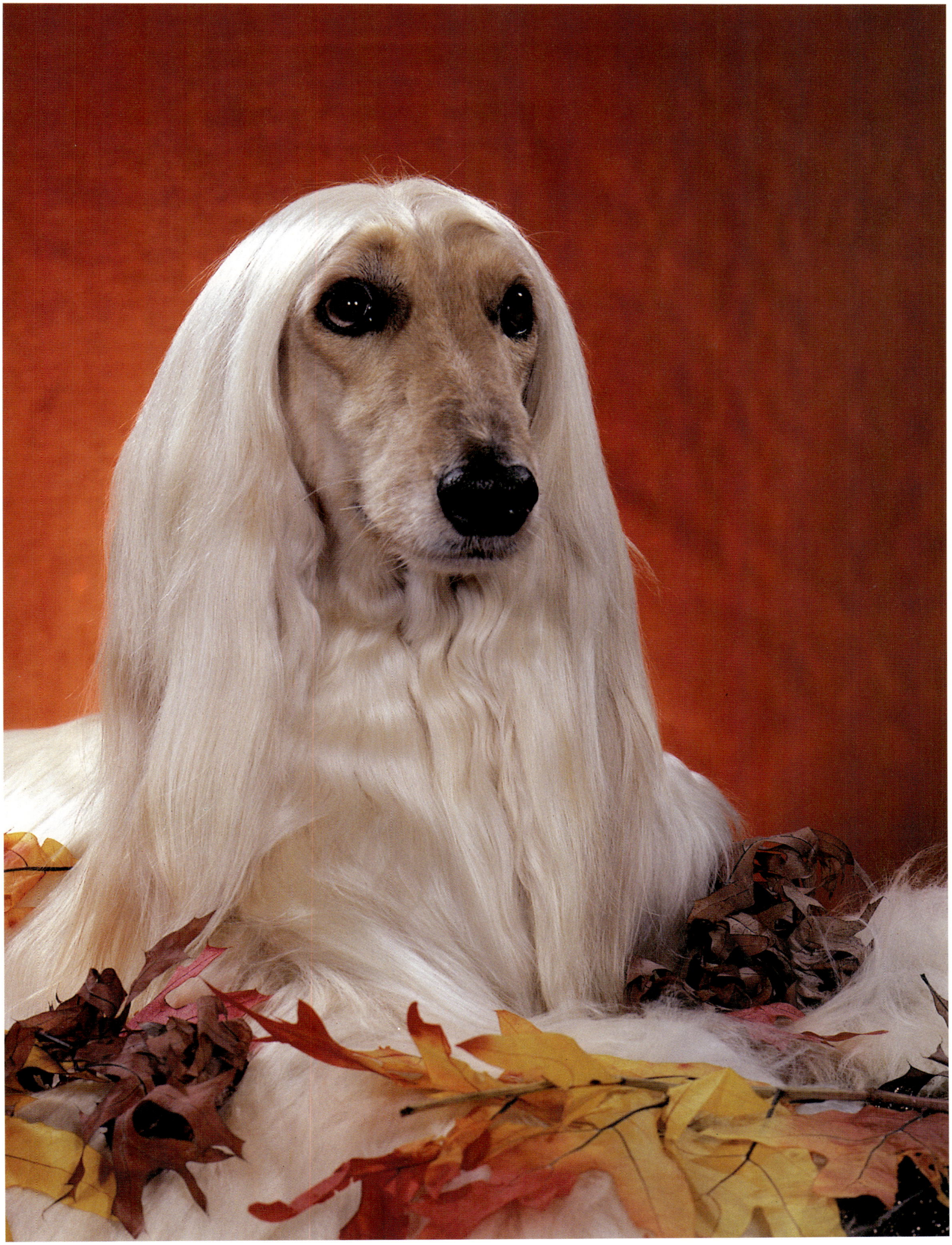

gian Elkhound, Otterhound, Pharaoh Hound, Rhodesian Ridgeback, Saluki, Whippet, Irish Wolfhound and Russian Wolfhound.

The Afghan resembles the Saluki in conformation, but has an entirely different and unique distribution of hair. The back and sides of the neck and face are sparsely covered, while the rest of the body has thick, silky hair.

The Greyhound was bred for coursing the hare and is used extensively for racing. It shows the correct form for speed in the dog, combining stamina and suppleness in perfect proportion. The breed stands as a tribute to fine breeding for a specialized purpose. The Whippet is a modified Greyhound, developed entirely for racing, although now it is often kept as a pet.

Below: A Saluki puppy.
Opposite: Born to run and bred to race, the Greyhound is the fastest of dogs.

55

Below: The Beagle, a loyal and faithful pet and companion, was originally bred as a hunting dog. Having roots in France, the breed was developed from stock that came to England with William the Conqueror in 1066.

Opposite: Like the Beagle, the sad-eyed Basset was born and bred to hunt.

The original purpose of the wolfhounds is apparent from their name. Now, however, they are used almost entirely as companions and guardians. The Russian Wolfhound, an aristocrat in bearing and appearance, could grace any castle, but the Irish Wolfhound is still thought in its original capacity. The tallest breed of dog, it is capable of lifting a wolf up by its scruff, yet its temperament is exceedingly gentle and tractable. These huge dogs need plenty of room to stretch their legs.

Beagles and Bassets are smaller hounds, traditionally bred for hunting hares and rabbits. These breeds typically accompanied hunters in packs, as can be seen in old prints of red-clad horsemen engaged in fox hunts. Beagles make lively little companions, but it was difficult to popularize the breed as house pets until Charles M Schultz introduced the popular comic strip character, Snoopy.

The names of many of the other hounds — Fox, Deer, Elk and Otter — describe what

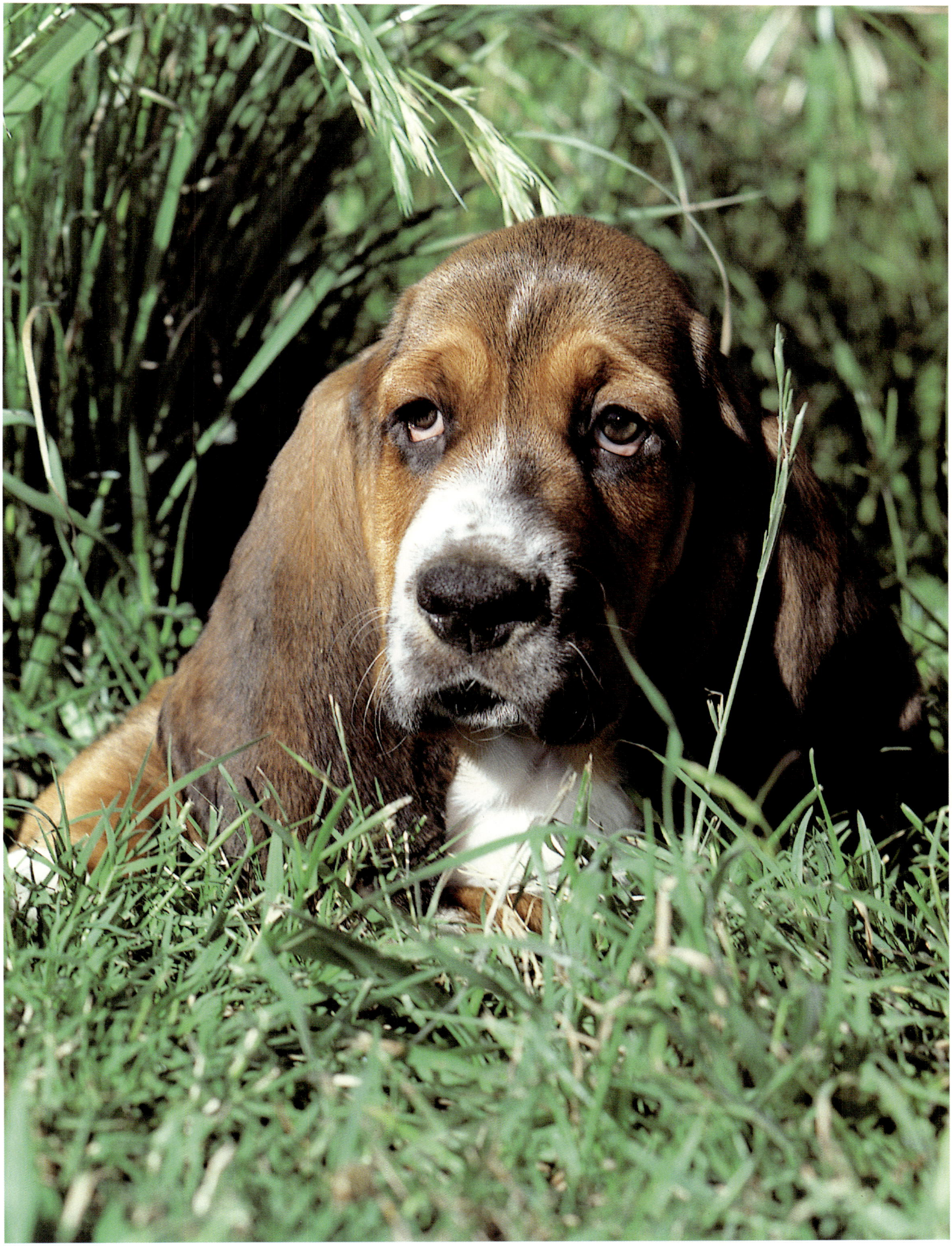

their traditional work was. The Norwegian Elkhound is more often seen as a pet than the others, while the Otterhound may claim some fame as one of the ancestors of the Airdale.

The Bloodhound, famous for its remarkable olfactory development, is used for tracking humans. This is probably the oldest of the hound breeds that hunts by scent. The name is misleading, for Bloodhounds are quite gentle, possessing what may be the saddest face in dogdom.

The Dachshund is popular as a house pet, being vivacious with lots of character. Highly intelligent, the Dachshund is a happy and busy little dog, especially if there is more than one in the household. It will always find something to do. Dachshund owners sometimes race the low-slung dogs. Bred for hunting badgers and foxes in Germany, the

Below: The Norwegian Elkhound is descended from hunting dogs bred by Vikings many centuries ago.
Opposite: The Bloodhound is a friendly and affectionate dog, bred for its acute sense of smell.

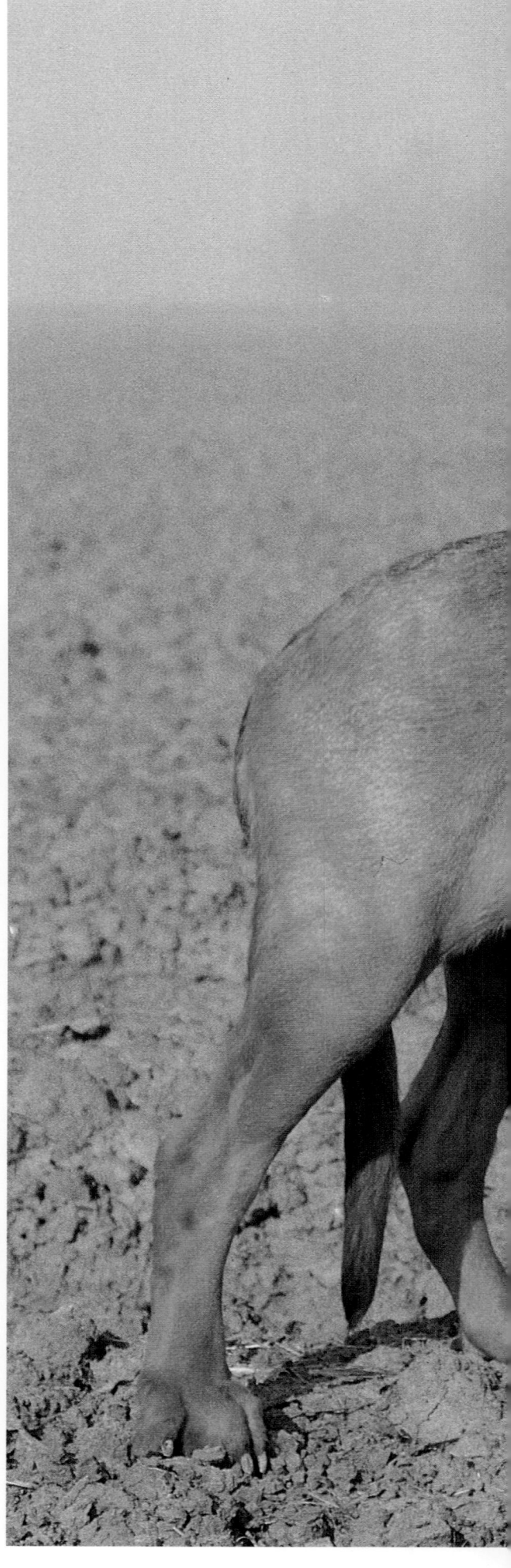

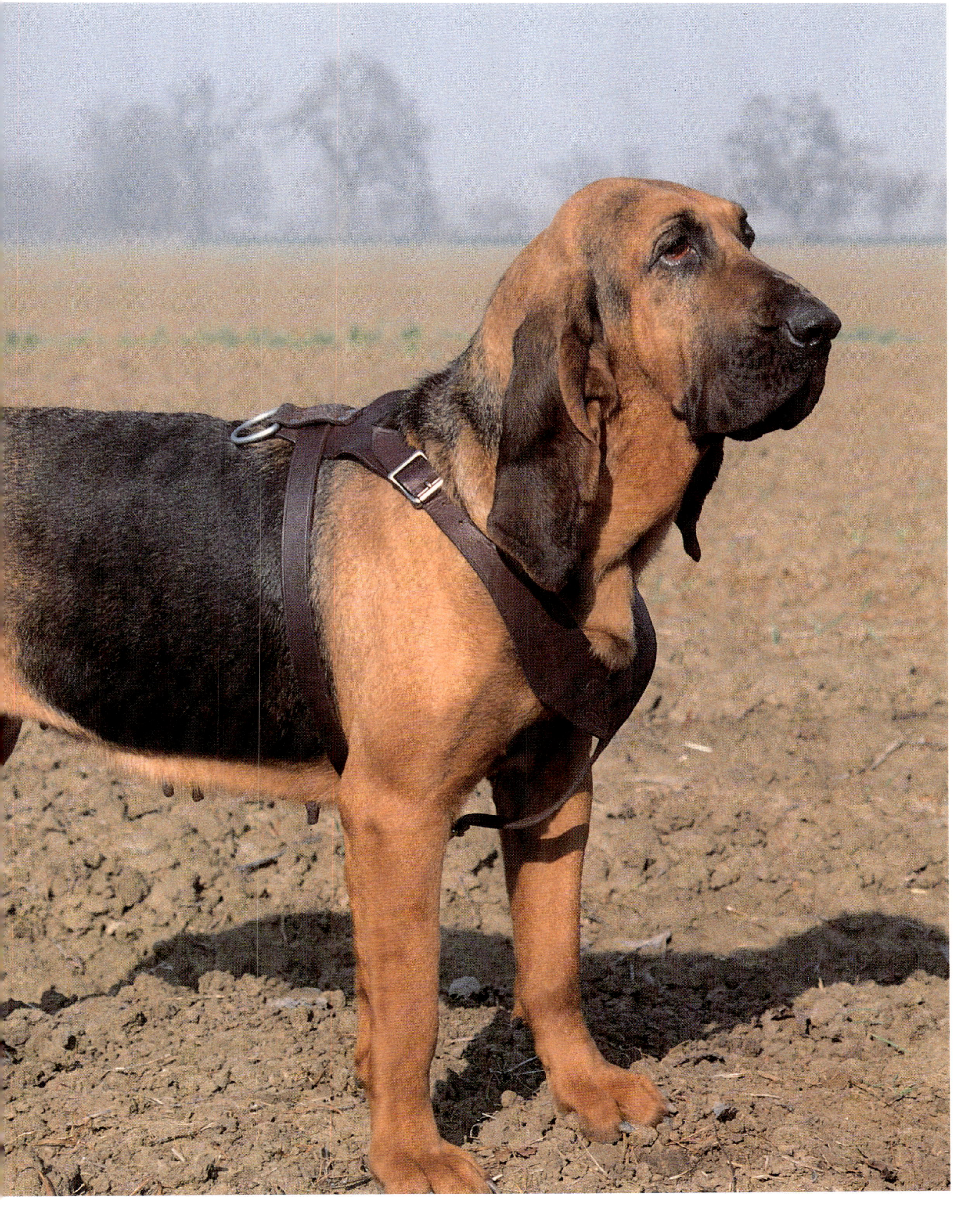

Below: A wire-haired Dachshund.
Right and opposite: Two long-haired Dachshunds. The breed, which originated in Germany, is known for its characteristic short legs and long ears, but it comes in a variety of coat types, from those pictured here, to short-haired.
Overleaf: Possessing the saddest face in the canine world, regardless of mood, the Basset Hound in the archetypical 'Hush puppy.'

'Doxie' is the only hound that will dig in. It comes in three varieties: Smooth, Wirehaired and Longhaired. The Smooth, or shorthaired, is the best known.

Hounds are all gentle and companionable, but not thought of as pets in the same sense as the dogs in the sporting group are. The Dachshund and the wolfhounds are probably most extensively seen as pets. There are no cropped ears in this group; the Elkhound is the only one having upright ears. The coats vary from the smooth, close type of the Greyhound to the long, silky kind seen on the Russian Wolfhound. There is also a wide range in size, from the Irish Wolf-hound's 150 pounds to the Dachshund's mere 15 pounds.

61

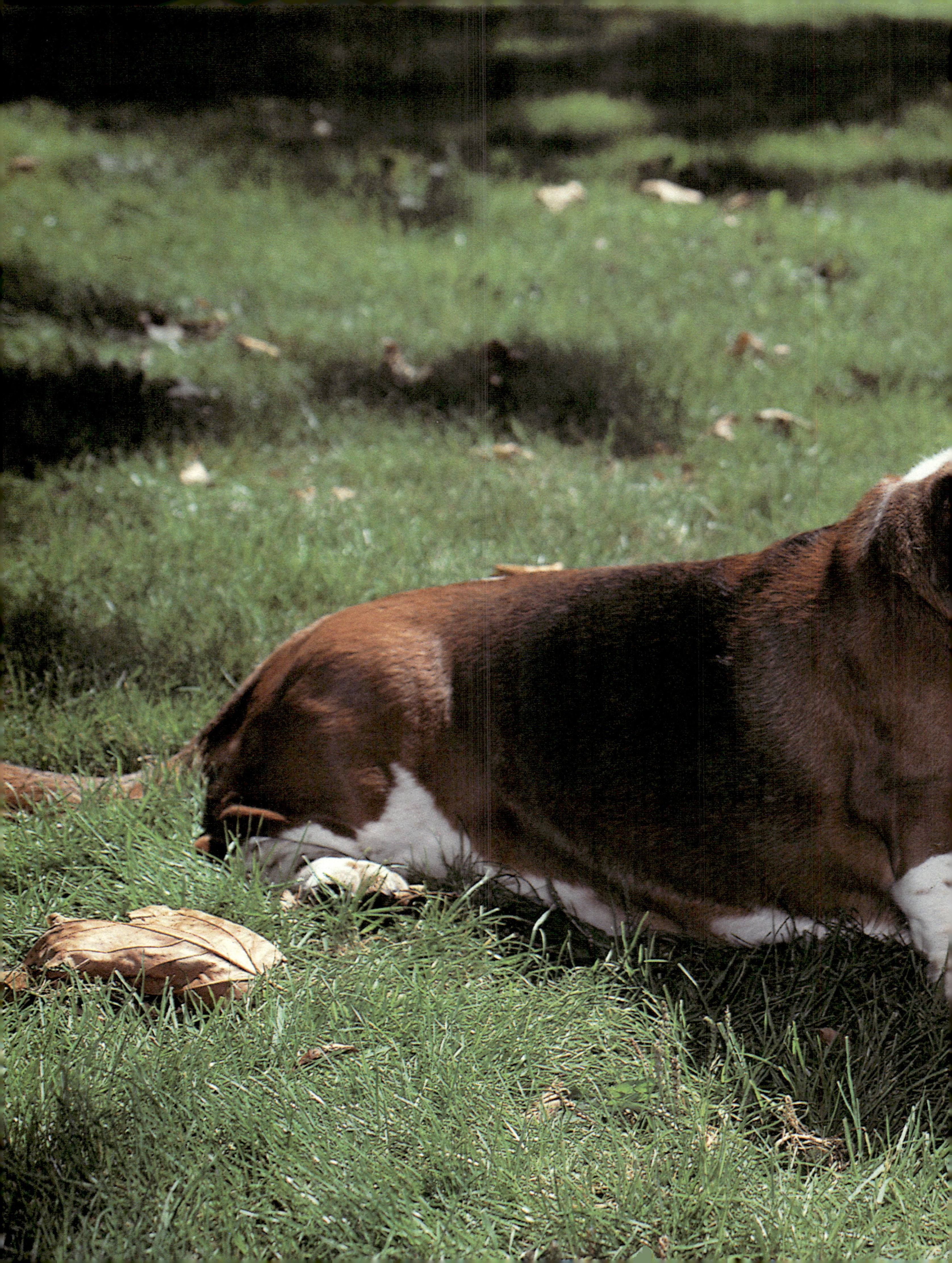

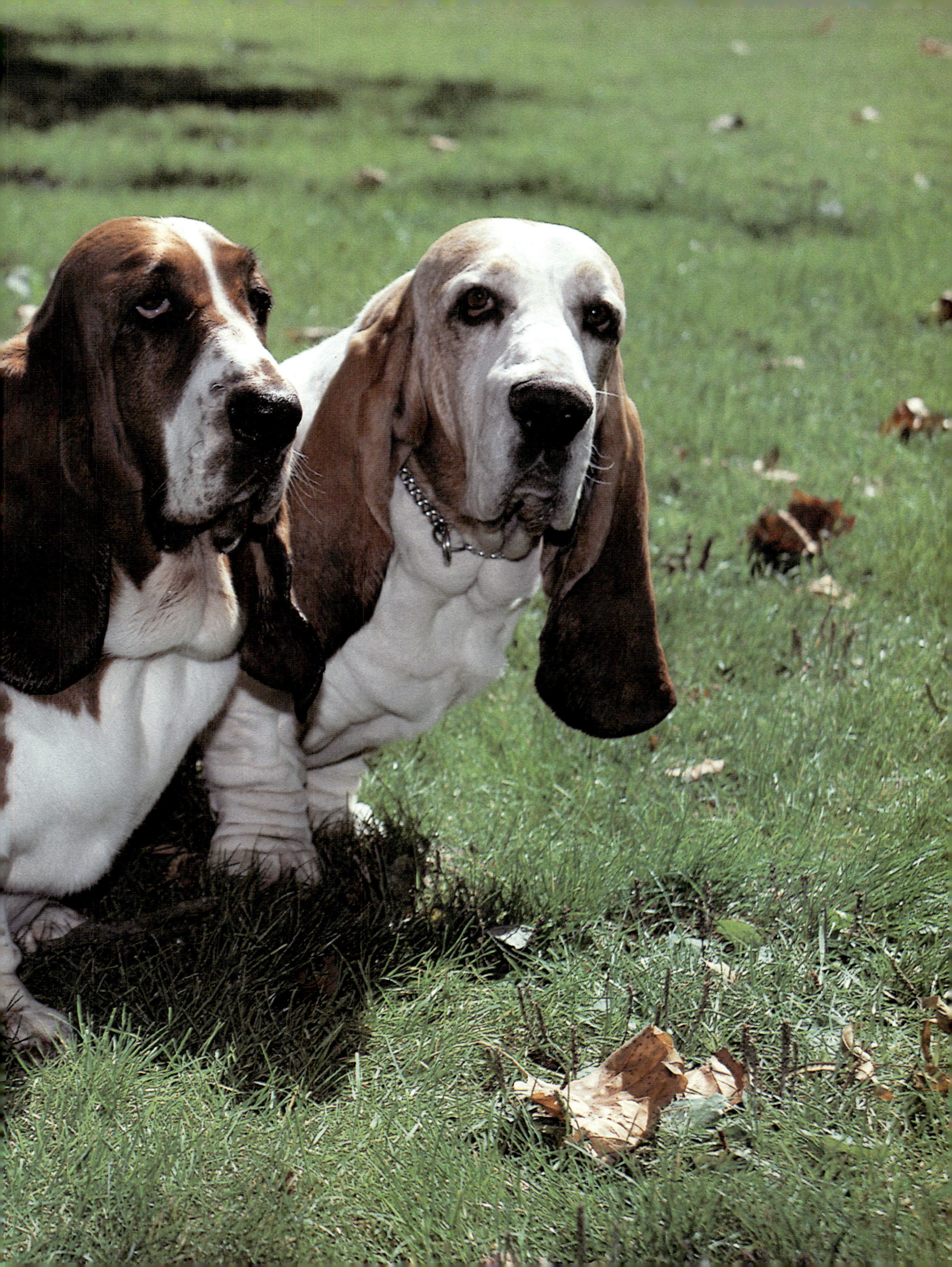

WORKING AND HERDING DOGS

Below: The Australian Cattle Dog is a typically hard-working breed.
Opposite: Highly prized in its native Japan, the Akita is descended from ancient hunting dogs.

The fearlessness so characteristic of the canine family reaches a high peak in these dogs, with their usefulness as protectors enhanced by their impressive size. Yet these dogs are also highly intelligent, and, with a strong hand, make excellent companions.

While all breeds of dogs can be loyal, trustworthy companians and useful in helping people, the dogs in this group are so-named because they have traditionally been used to assist people in their daily lives.

They are associated with the more practical, work-oriented aspects of life, although their original purposes are mostly overlooked in our present modes of living. They were all developed for some definite purpose and, in their ability to perform certain work, are as specialized as the sporting dogs are for their own duties. In addition to each's particular utility, they are all excellent guardians of person and property. The breeds include the Akita, Bernese Mountain Dog, Boxer, Bullmastiff, Doberman Pinscher, Great Dane,

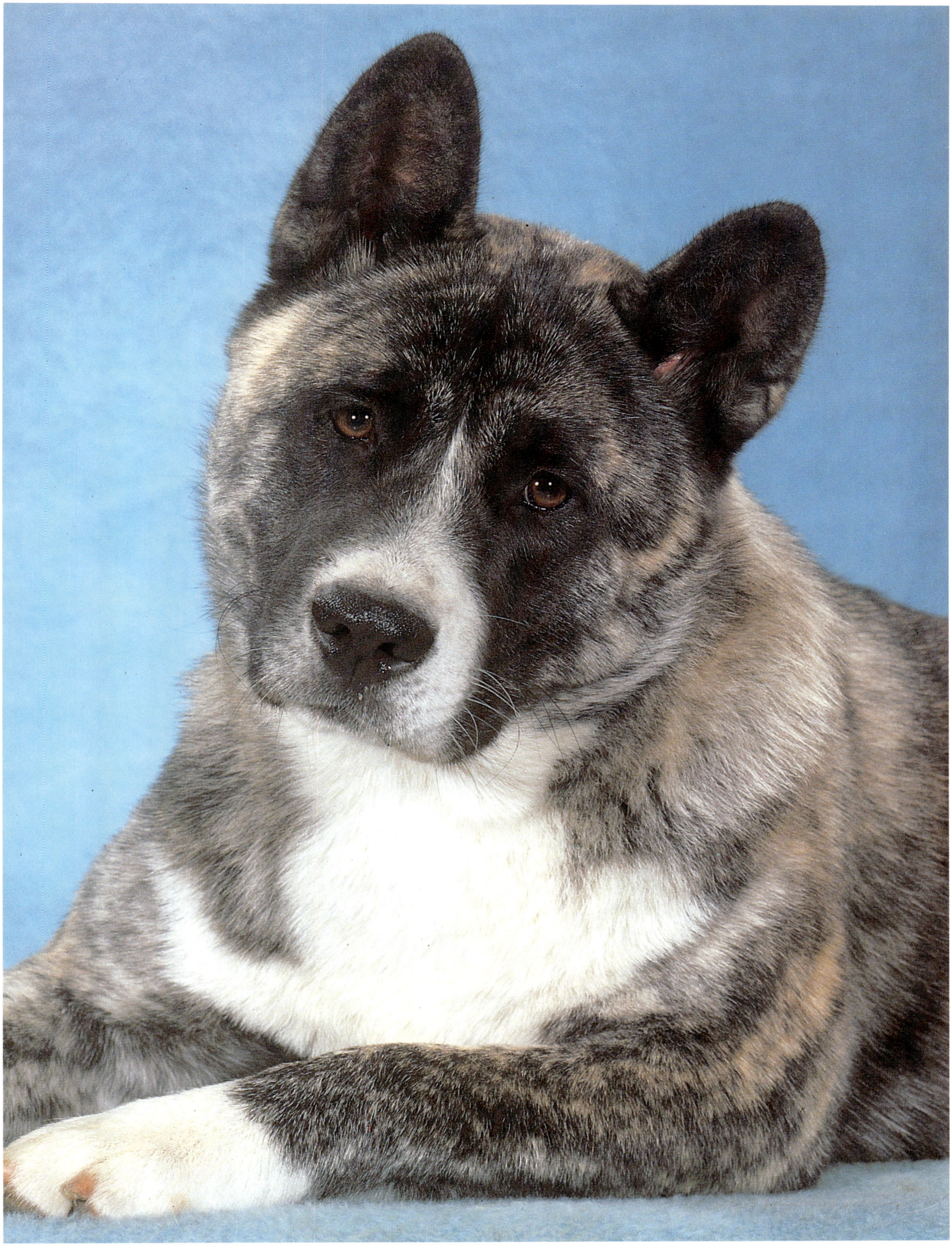

Great Pyrenees, Komondor, Alaskan Malamute, Mastiff, Newfoundland, Portuguese Water Dog, Rottweiler, St Bernard, Samoyed, Giant Schnauzer, Standard Schnauzer and Siberian Husky.

In addition to dogs bred to be guardians, specific breeds have been developed for helping people herd livestock. Centuries of assisting humans have imbued the herding dogs with a sense of responsibility that is reflected in their manner. If the proper environment can be provided, they make devoted pets and are highly recommended. The breeds of this group are intelligent and exhibit a resourcefulness that enables them to work out the solutions to various problems without their owner's aid.

The herding dogs are the Australian Cattle Dog, Australian Sheepdog, Bearded Collie, Belgian Malinois, Belgian Sheepdog, Belgian Tervuren, Bouviers des Flandres, Briard, Collie, German Shepherd, Great Pyrenees, Komondor, Kuvasz, Old English Sheepdog, Pulik, Shetland Sheepdog and Welsh Corgis (Cardigan and Pembroke). Sometimes called the pastoral group, they are best known for their herding instincts.

The Doberman, Rottweiler and Giant Schnauzer are of German origin and served primarily as guardians for farms. The last two were sometimes referred to as 'butcher dogs,' or guardians of butchers' wagons. They all have docked tails, and the Schnauzer and Doberman have cropped ears as well. They retain the traits which made them so valuable in the past: aggressive when necessary, yet gentle and devoted companions to their owners. The Schnauzer family also

Below: A happy and loveable Great Pyrenees.
Opposite: Looking determined and purposeful, this Miniature Schnauzer mother is protective of her pup. She is typical of the breed, which was developed in Germany as a cross between the Schnauzer and the Affenpinscher.

67

includes the standard and miniature sizes which are similar to, but smaller than the Giant Schnauzer. The Standard Schnauzer makes a good, general companion and stands from about 17 to 20 inches. The miniature has the same points, but is six inches smaller.

The Doberman Pinscher, being especially keen and highly intelligent, is the most popular of the trio. It was bred by Louis Dobermann between 1865 and 1870. Herr Dobermann was also a tax collector as well as the keeper of the local animal shelter. He needed a large, strong and agile dog to protect him while he was out collecting taxes. Bred to be guard dogs, it is common for two month old puppies to snarl and show their teeth. Gottfried Lietchi, a Swiss breeder, said: 'They were certainly robust, had absolutely no fear, not even of the devil himself, and it required a great deal of courage to own one.'

The Doberman has served not only as a guard dog, but also as a police dog, a military patrol dog and a guide dog for the blind. The 'Dobe' was adopted by the US Marines as their official war dog during World War II. During that war, a Doberman named Andy was decorated for sniffing out two hidden machine gun nests and saving a tank platoon in Bougainville.

There is an often told story of a particularly ferocious-looking Doberman that won Best in Show three times before a brave judge finally pried the dog's mouth open and discovered that it was missing several teeth — a serious flaw. This short-coated dog of sleek beauty has gained a host of friends and admirers with its unassuming manner and protective qualities. The Doberman is well adapted to training and is still extensively used for security.

The Rottweiler is believed to have crossed the Alps from Italy to Southern Germany with the Roman soldiers. In the Middle Ages, these large dogs were used to drive cattle to market. In addition to their herding duties, Rottweilers were used to pull carts and as guard dogs and companions. Today they are used in security, military and police

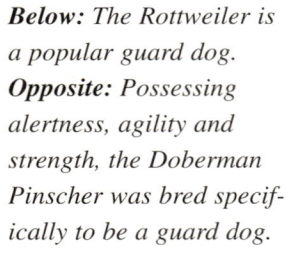

Below: The Rottweiler is a popular guard dog.
Opposite: Possessing alertness, agility and strength, the Doberman Pinscher was bred specifically to be a guard dog.

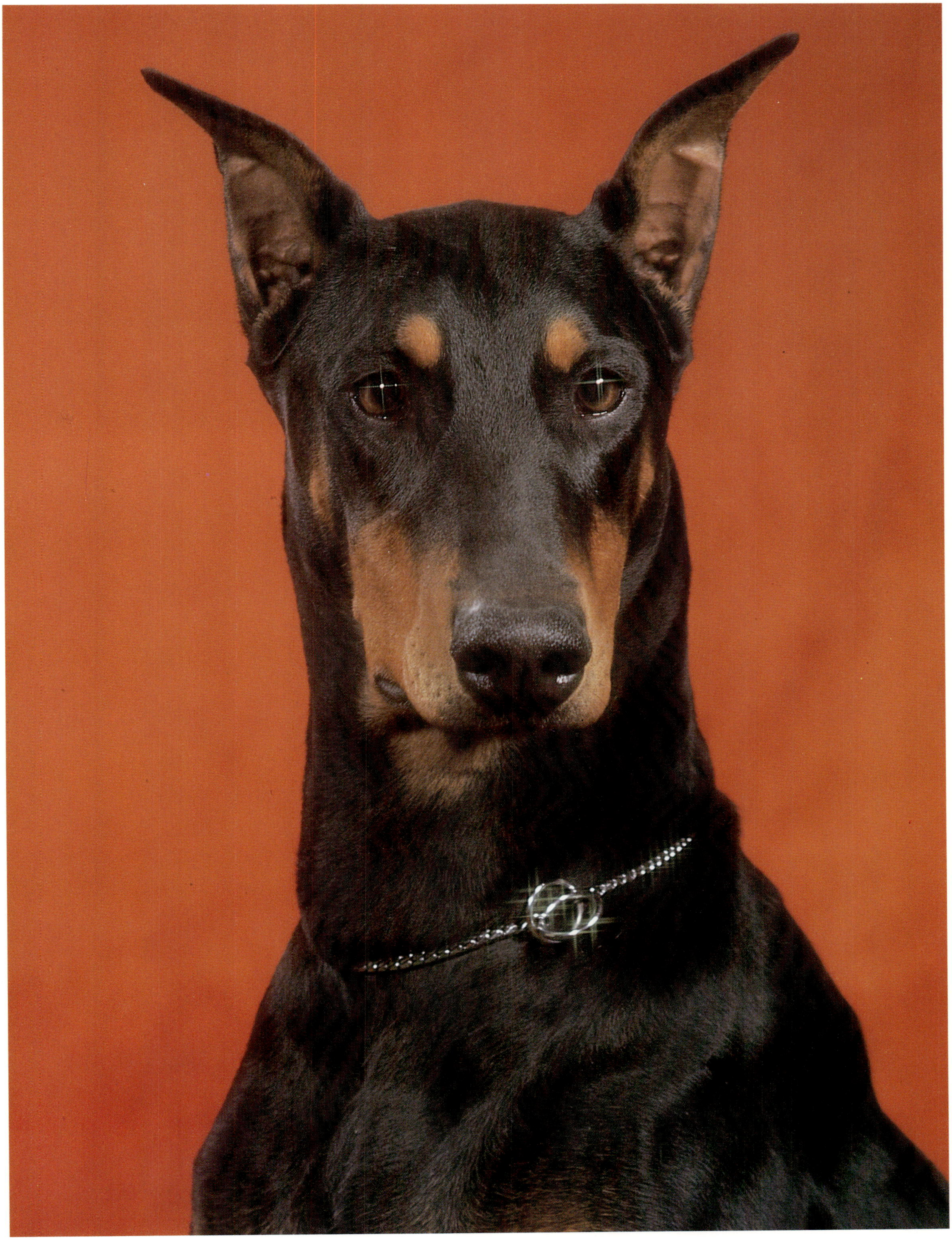

work. While not an excitable dog, the breed is very defensive and aggressive toward both canine and human strangers.

The Husky, Alaskan Malamute and Samoyed are the dogs that the native Inuit people, as well as explorers, depended upon in the snow and ice of the Arctic and Antarctic. They are sled dogs, although in northern Siberia the Samoyed is used to herd reindeer for the Samoyed people. These breeds are characterized by compactness, muscular development and a heavy coat. Their coloring is any of the accepted dog colors, except for the Samoyed, who is white, white and biscuit or cream. The Eskimo and Alaskan Malamute can weigh as much as 85 pounds, the Siberian Husky, up to 64 pounds, and the Samoyed, 55 pounds as a maximum.

Among the most popular of the large guardian dogs is the Great Dane. This huge, regal-looking animal should never be less than 30 inches high and comes in fawn, brindle, blue or harlequin. For centuries the Great Dane was bred for wild-boar hunting, and has even been used for draft purposes. Today it is considered most effective and valuable as a companion and protector. It is short coated and has cropped ears.

Boxers are of German origin, originally bred for police work, and have docked tails

Below: An endearing little Siberian Husky pup. *Opposite:* Like its near relative, the Husky, the Alaskan Malamute has had a long and important career as a sled dog.

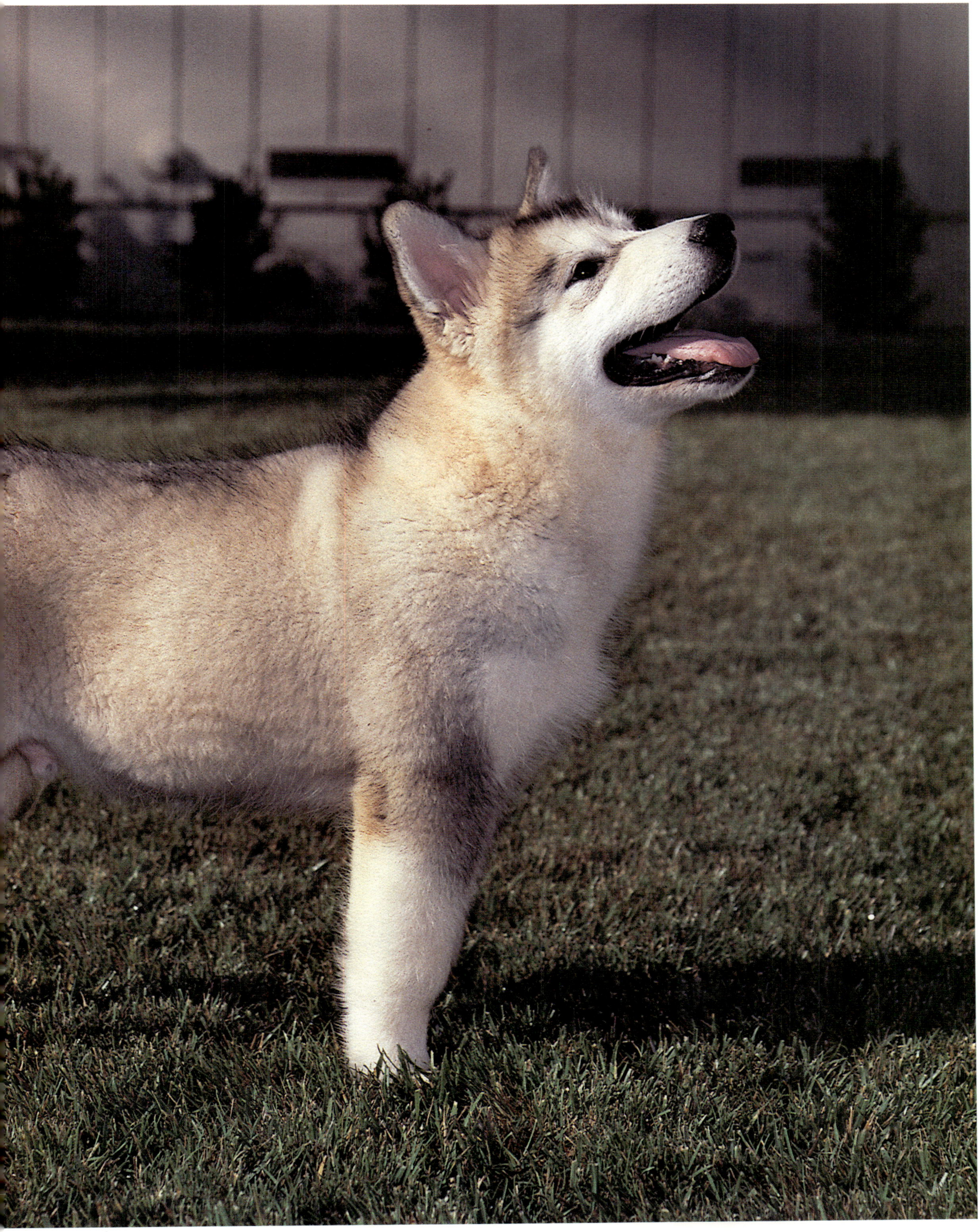

and cropped ears. They are large — up to about 24 inches for males — stocky, fearless, and make good companions and guardians. They have been used as guide dogs for the blind. During both World Wars, Boxers were medical aides, messengers and protectors. The trained Boxer is businesslike without being obtrusive, and their short, usually brindle-colored coat is easily maintained. Potentially boisterous and stubborn, they require a firm hand in training.

The Mastiff and Bullmastiff fall within the group of guardians, assuming the work naturally. Both are huge, short-coated dogs, of either a fawn or brindle color, with black masks and ears. Despite their muscular development, they are aristocratic in bearing. Both have endeared themselves to many with their docile manner, yet they can become thoroughly formidable if the need arises. The Mastiff is the oldest of the British dogs. They were found in England by Roman invaders, who took them home to fight lions in their arenas. In the Elizabethan period, they were kept to bait bears and lions; the rules of the alleged sport required three mastiffs to be sent against a bear and four against a lion. The Bullmastiff comes from a Bulldog-Mastiff cross.

One descendant of the Mastiff-like dogs brought to Helvetia by the Roman legions is

Below: The Great Dane is a large and muscular breed that originated in Europe as hunting dog.
Right: An eastern Russian native, the Samoyed is a cousin of the Husky and Malamute.
Opposite: The square jaw and distinctive muzzle are the characteristic features of the Boxer.

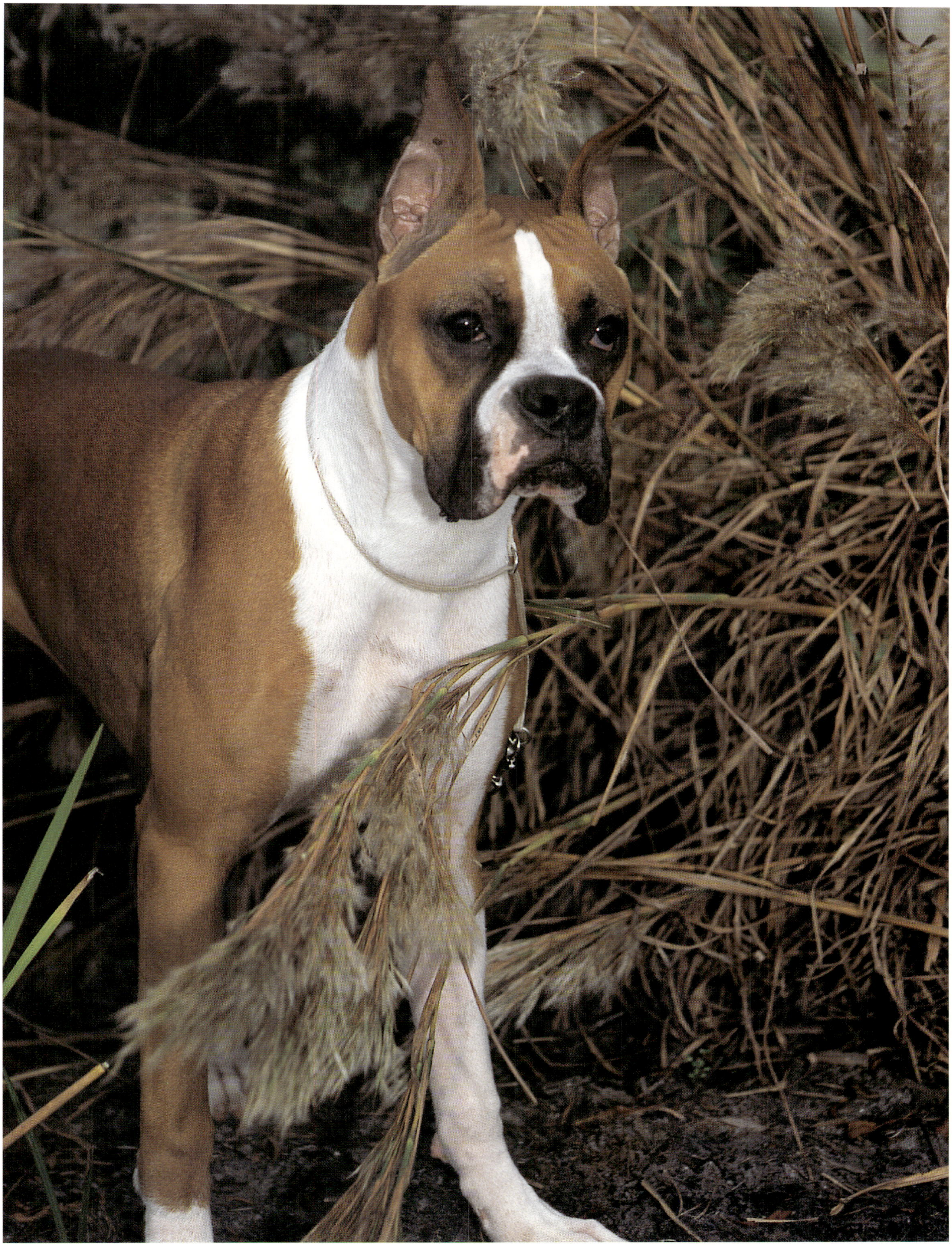

the Bernese Mountain Dog. A cousin of the St Bernard, the Bernese Mountain Dog had nearly died out by the late 1800s. The breed was saved by two Swiss dog fanciers, Franz Schertenlieb and Professor Albert Heim.

The Newfoundland and St Bernard are old breeds and have a very colorful background. The English poet George Byron inscribed upon the gravestone of his Newfoundland, Boatswain, 'Beauty without vanity, Strength without insolence, Courage without ferocity, and all the Virtues of man without his vices.' The saving of human life is more or less instinctive in any breed, but it has probably attained its highest form in these two breeds. The all-black and black-and-white Newfoundland and the red-and-white St Bernards have a dignified bearing and a gentle, unruffled manner. Their facial expressions reveal sagacity and kindness and, if it were possible, everyone would like to own at least one of these wonderful dogs. Unfortunately, their large size prevents a more general distribution of both breeds.

The Portuguese Water Dog was specifically bred to swim. Some dogs like to swim, but the Portuguese Water Dog was bred and trained to pull nets and fish from the sea. They also dived into the water, catching escaped fish in their mouths and bringing them back to the boat or shore. In addition, these dogs were messengers between boats. A large and powerfully built dog, the Portuguese Water Dog has a thick, curly coat and webbed feet. These dogs do not shed and are great family dogs. The ideal owner will, of course, provide this active dog with a place to run and swim.

The Belgian Sheepdog and its cousin, the Belgian Tervuren, resemble in many respects the German Shepherd, a very familiar breed. The Bouvier des Flandres is another breed of Belgian sheepherder and general farm dog. He is taller than the other Belgian sheepdogs, and has cropped ears and tail. The Briard is an old breed of French farm dog used in a variety of ways and is about the same size as the Bouvier.

Below: With origins in Switzerland, the Bernese Mountain Dog is an extremely handsome breed.

Left: The Belgian Tervueren is a handsome shepherd breed which originated in Belgium in the 1890s.
Below: A lovely litter of St Bernard puppies.

Dogs may come and go, but the good old reliable Collie still remains a favorite. The Collie is probably the best known of the sheepherding dogs and comes in two forms: Rough and Smooth coated. The Smooth Collie is not commonly seen in the United States. The Collie, developed in the Scottish Highlands, is the backbone of the sheep industry in Great Britain. The Collie is able to do the work of a dozen men, running to a distant pasture, rounding up the flock, separating out individuals, gathering up stragglers and bringing them all home, guarding against predators the entire time. The instincts of the Collie remain the same, even if the coat has been improved. The children may not always enjoy it, but the Collie considers it great fun to gather them for lunch, herding the toddlers and gathering the stragglers attempting to make a break for the street.

The Collie has been a favorite of Hollywood for many years. The most famous movie Collie is, of course, Lassie. The orig-

Below and opposite: The coat of the Collie may vary in length and can be smooth or rough. The Collie is one of the more popular herding breeds.

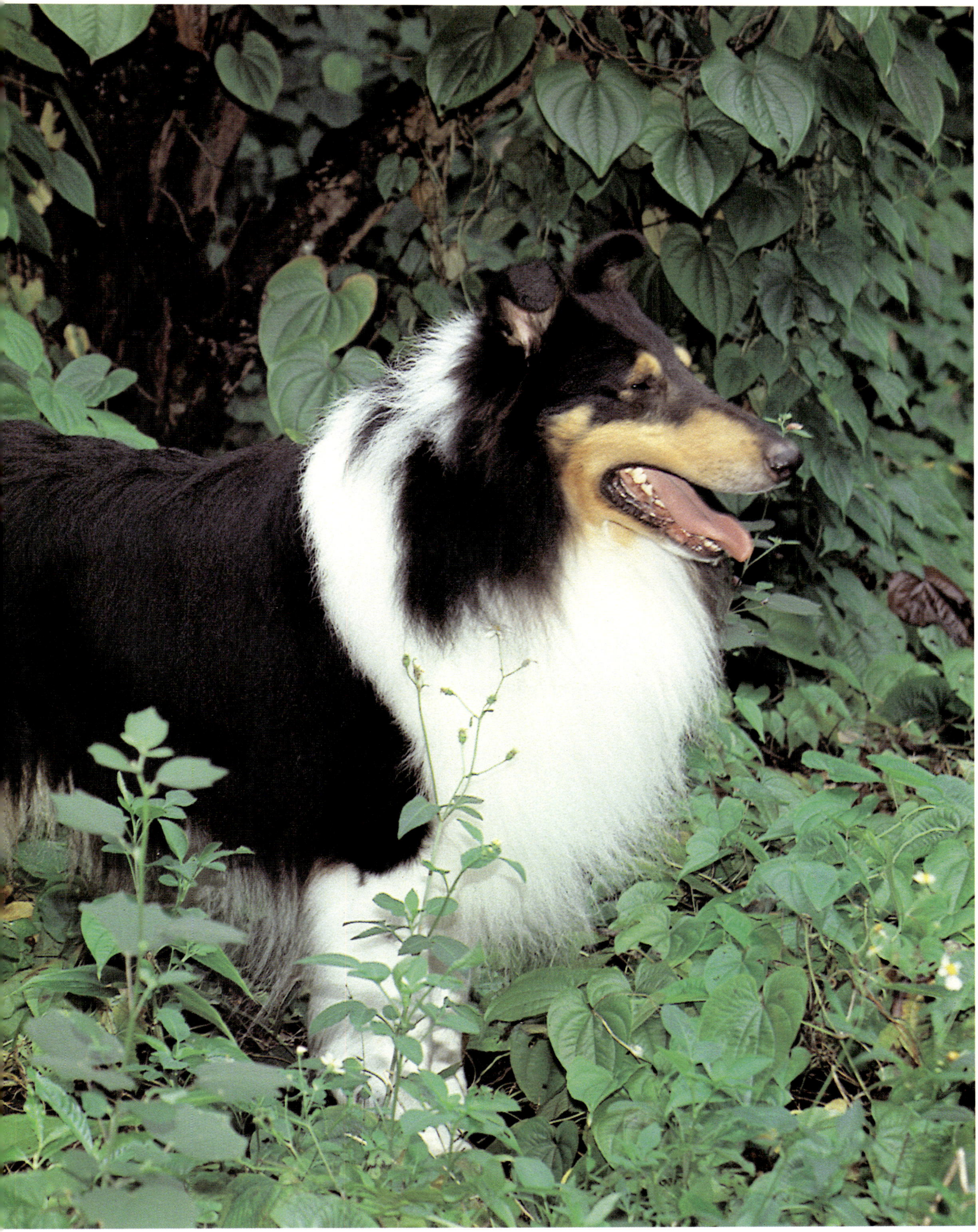

inal Lassie was a male dog named Pal, recruited from over 300 candidates to play the heroine in *Lassie Come Home*. There have been at least eight 'Lassie' movies — including the important film simply entitled *Lassie* that was released in 1994 — as well as a radio show, a television series airing from 1954 to 1972 and an animated cartoon version.

Like the Collie, the Shetland Sheepdog traces its ancestry back to the Border Collie of Scotland. The Shetland Sheepdog is, in effect, a miniature Rough Collie and possesses the same temperament. It is popular with those who admire the Collie, but wish for a smaller dog. An affectionate family dog, the Shetland Sheepdog was originally bred to be a working dog and requires a large yard and lots of attention.

The German Shepherd, also known as the German police dog, scarcely needs a description. This is a general all-round dog — herding was their original purpose, but their performance in war and police work have brought them to the attention of the world. They are excellent guide dogs, military patrol dogs, police dogs and watchdogs. While

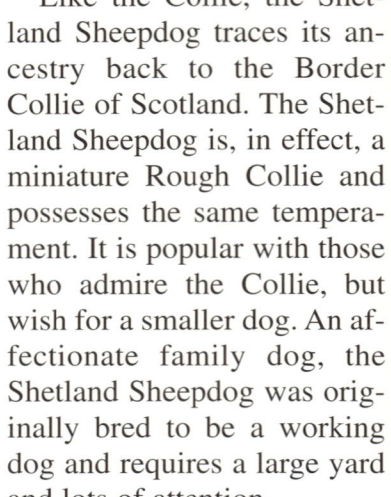

Below: One of the world's finest sheepdogs, the Border Collie was introduced into Scotland by the Vikings in the eighth century.

Right and opposite: The Shetland Sheepdog closely resembles its cousin, the Collie.

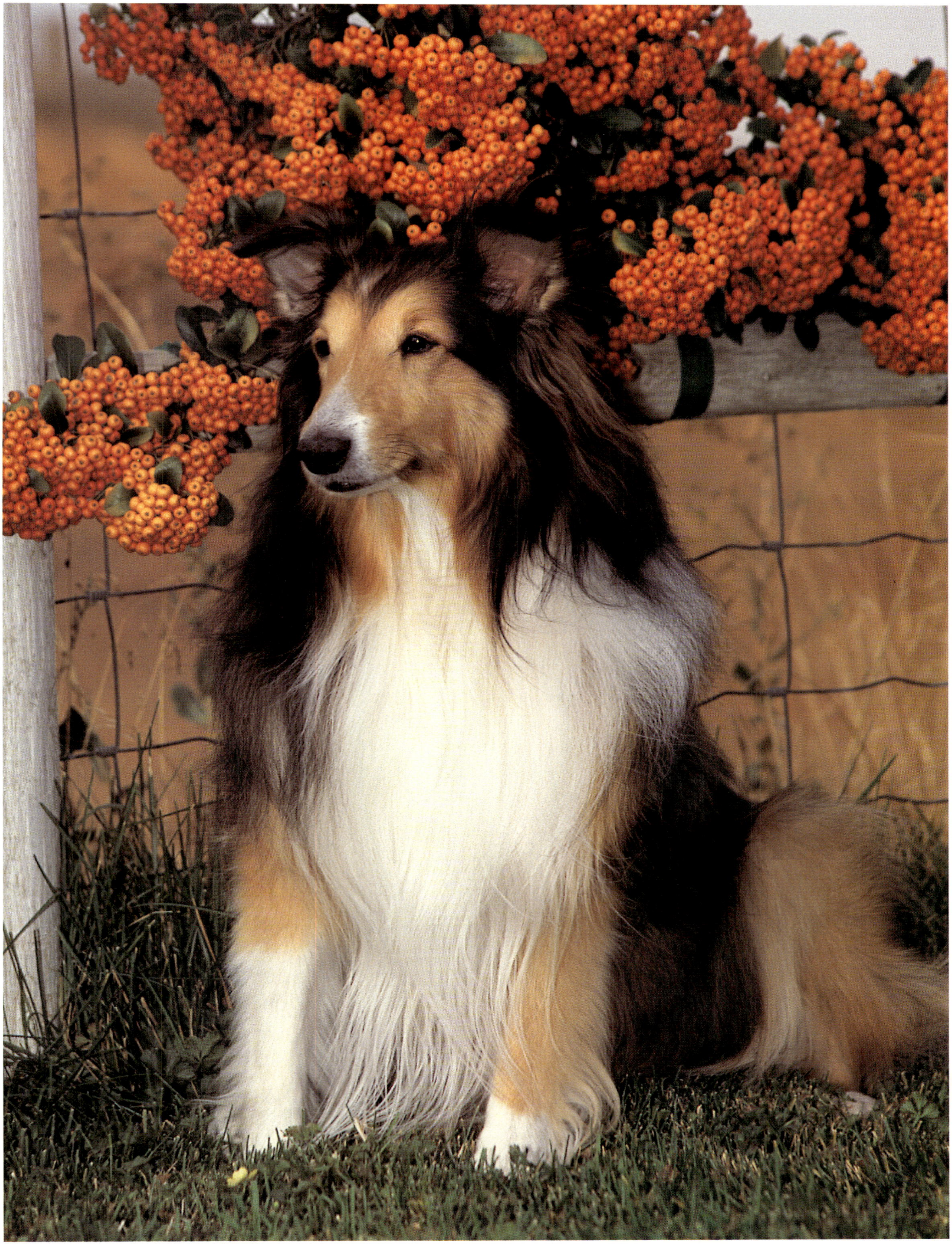

still a favorite breed, an immense demand for them began after World War I. Despite their stern appearance, the German Shepherd loves working with people and is eager to please. It is a good family dog, very protective of children and hostile toward strange dogs and humans. The dog is active and requires a very large space and human companionship.

A recent incident in Downey, California exemplifies the German Shepherd's personality. KC, the Griffith family's dog, allows the grandchildren to ride her like a horse and is never happier than when a little one is 'petting' her (pounding with little fists on her back.) KC was in the backyard at about 4 am when she started barking. Mrs Griffith got up and told KC to be quiet. Shortly afterward KC started barking loudly again. Then flashlights began shining into the kitchen windows. When Mrs Griffith demanded to know who was outside, a voice said 'Downey Police Department,' and requested that she take KC inside. The officers, searching for a robbery suspect with another German Shepherd,

Below and opposite: The German Shepherd, which, as its name implies, originated in Germany as a shepherd, is also a popular guard dog. The black nose is a defining characteristic.

had jumped over the Griffiths' fence. When they met KC, they were forced to stay where they were until she was removed from the yard. While she did not attack the officers, she was determined that they were not going through her yard. Yet, when called inside, KC obeyed. The suspect apparently did try to escape through the yard but was forced to balance on a cement block wall between the houses — trapped between KC and the neighbor's German Shepherd!

The Old English Sheepdog is a shaggy coated, bobtailed animal of distinctive appearance, originally bred for cold climates.

Below: Having originated in Hungary, the mop-like Komondor is a popular sheep dog that resembles the sheep that it is typically used to herd.
Bottom and opposite: The Welsh Corgi is Queen Elizabeth's favorite breed.

Their ambling gait and conformation somehow suggest a bear. The breed is most gentle and affectionate. The Great Pyrenees is a large, white dog from the Pyrenees. Some Pyrenees are as large as Great Danes and have been used for hundreds of years in their native land. The Kuvasz, from Hungary, is large, white, and beautiful. He is often called the Hungarian Sheepdog, although this may prove somewhat misleading as there are two other breeds of sheep dogs in Hungary: the Komondor and Pulik.

The Welsh Corgi is classed with the herding dogs, although their real job was to repel the animals that trespassed into their owner's domain. This is the smallest of the group, and it measures about 12 inches at the shoulder. There

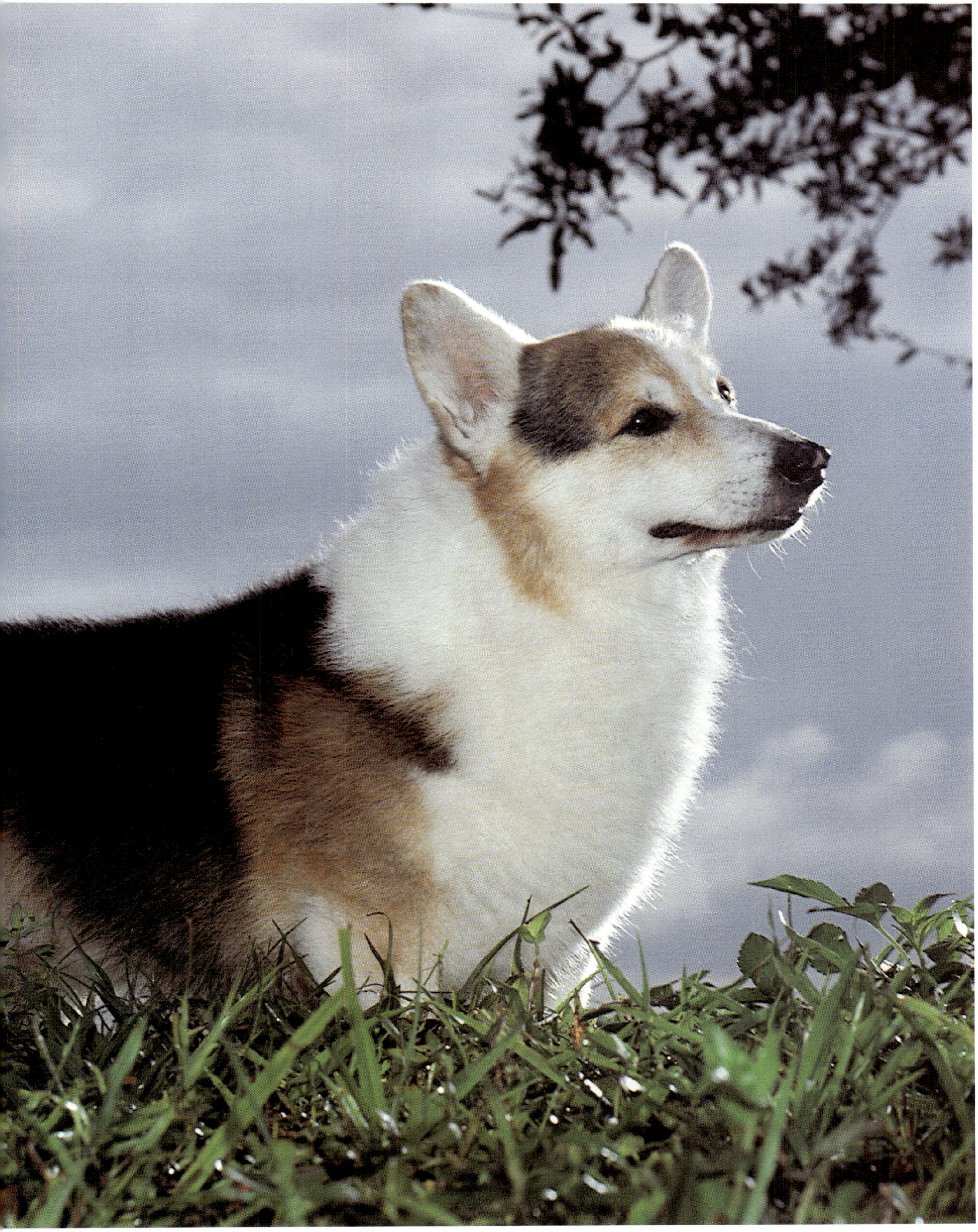

Below: The Australian Cattle Dog was originally bred to herd cattle across the Australian outback.
Opposite: An Australian Shepherd.
Overleaf: A young Shetland Sheepdog.

are two recognized forms of the Welsh Corgi: Pembroke and Cardigan. The most readily discernible difference to the average person is in the tails of these dogs: the Pembroke has a short tail and the Cardigan has a long one, similar to a fox's. Both dogs have a foxy appearance. Queen Elizabeth has loved the Welsh Corgis since she was a child and has done much to popularize the dogs in Great Britain.

The breeds that originated in Australia were developed using the Collie and the native species, the dingo. With this base stock, the Australians bred several excellent herding dogs, including the Australian Shepherd and the Australian Cattle Dog. Quick, agile and intelligent, both breeds are supreme 'escape artists.' They are very active, requiring a lot of attention, and are often the classic 'one man (or woman) dog.'

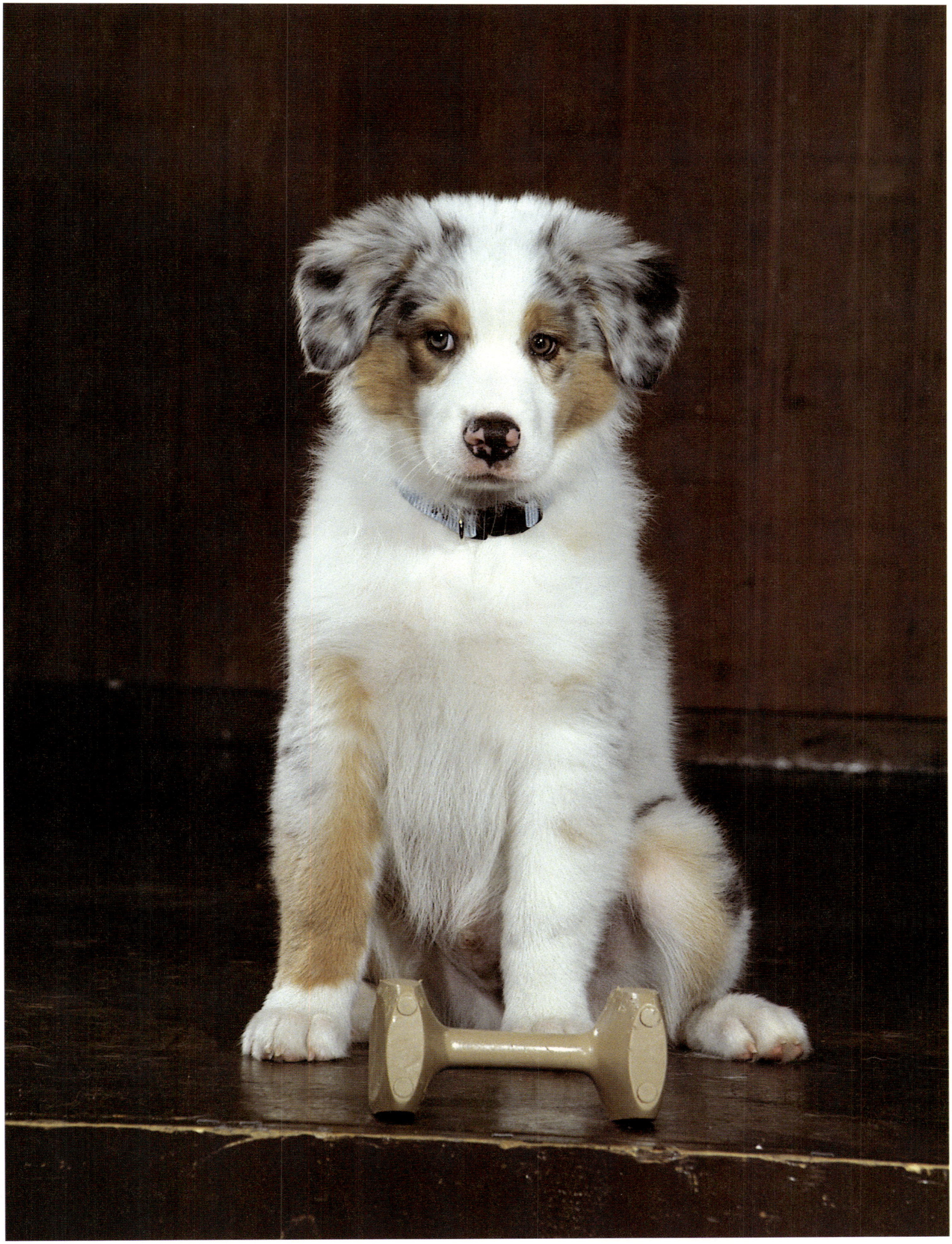

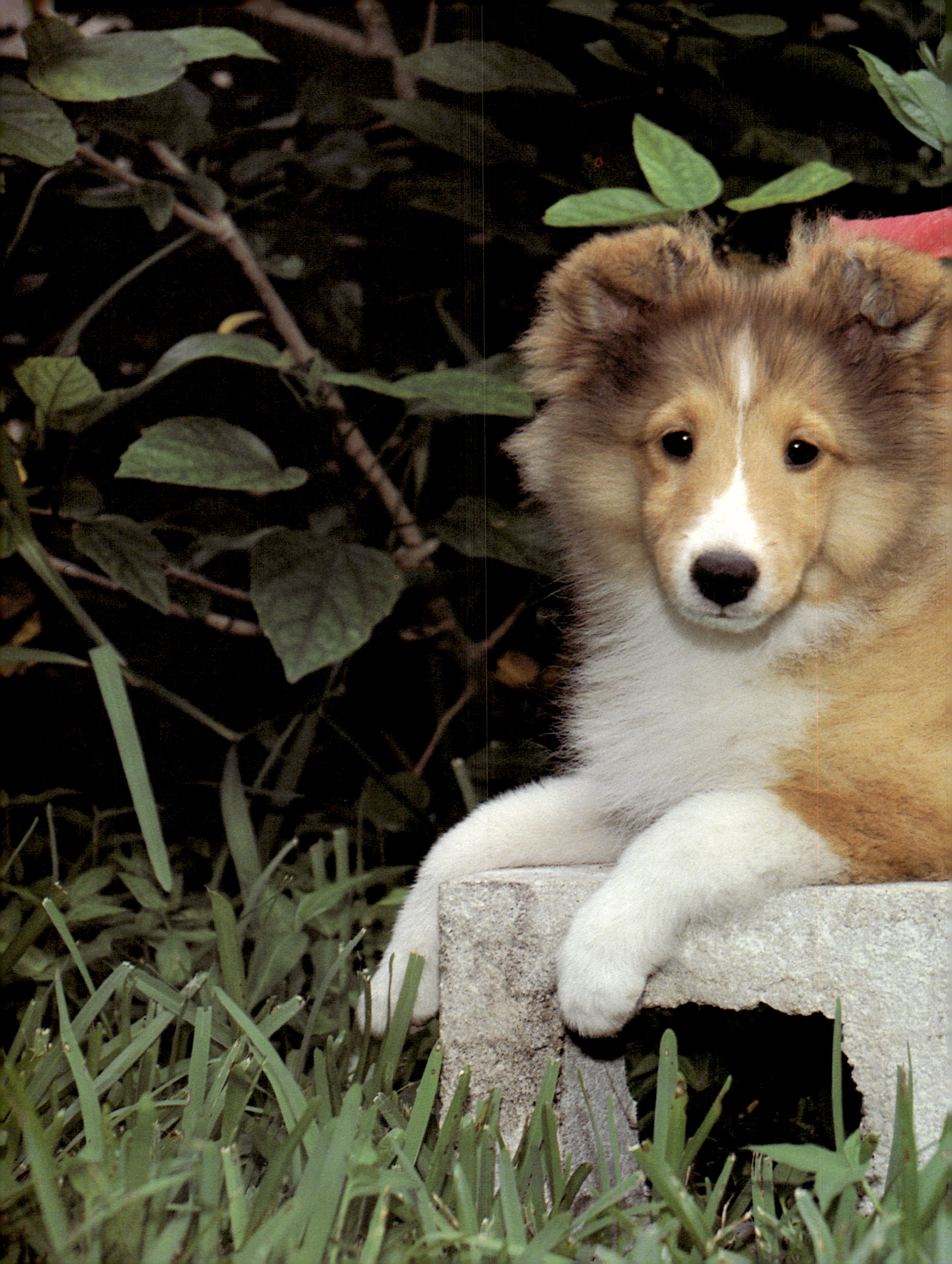

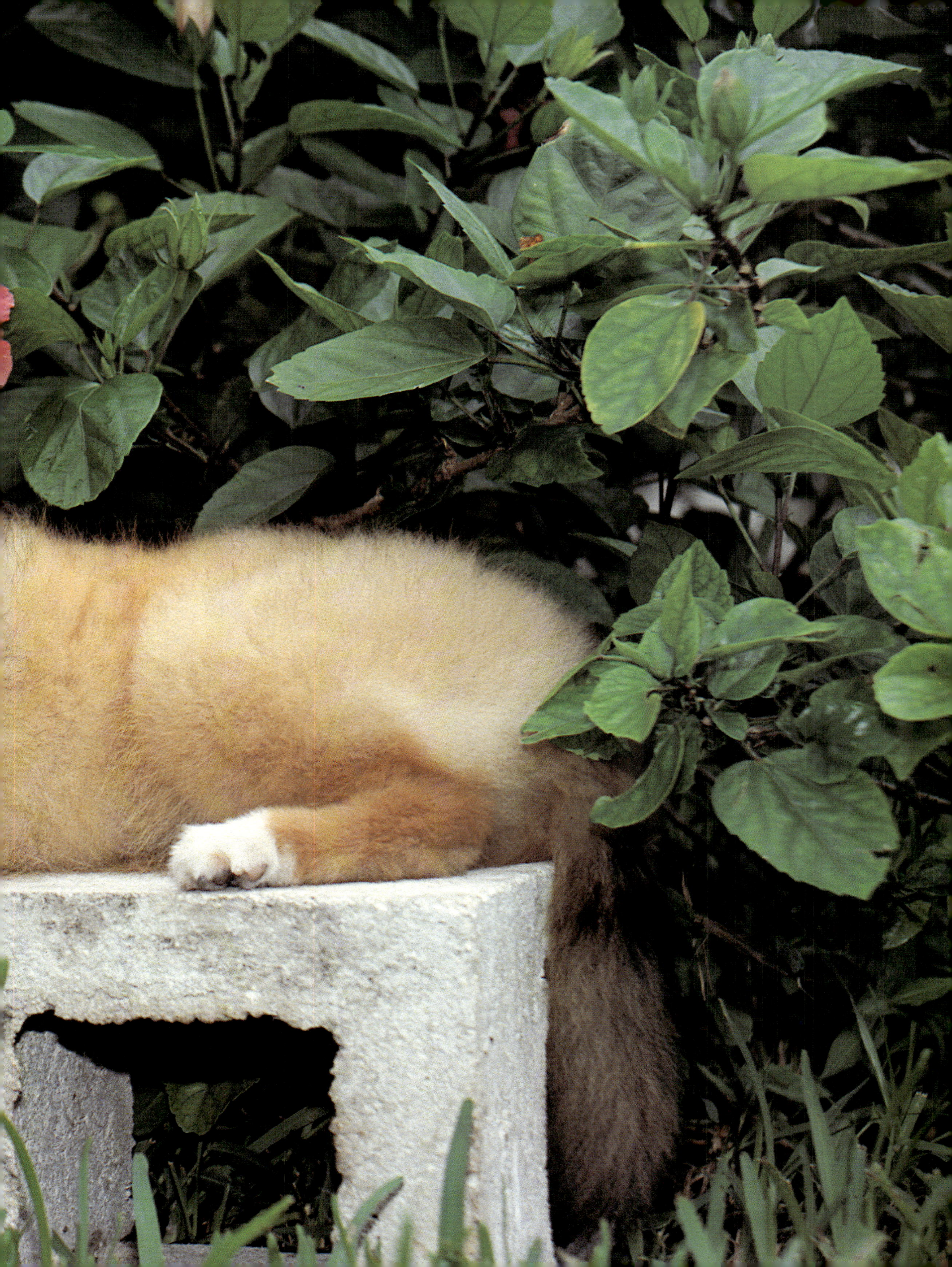

TOYS

Below and opposite: The smallest canine breed, the Chihuahua is a descendant of small dogs that were indigenous to Central America and domesticated by the Mayans.

Close companionship with humans for many centuries has made the toy dogs understanding, sympathetic and intuitive. They are invariably pert, intelligent and self-assertive. Their size, beauty and apparent helplessness bring them considerable attention. In some cases, this works to the detriment of the animal, as many dogs are petted and pampered to the breaking point, often becoming thoroughly spoiled. Some have terrier instincts, which they are prevented from indulging because of their size. They adapt themselves well to a home environment and can be kept where outdoor activities are necessarily limited.

To many, these little fellows seem to be unnecessary members of the canine family, and their very existence is looked upon with intolerance. There is no reason for such a feeling. The toys have a charm and comprehension far out of proportion to their size, and have given immeasurable pleasure to many thousands all over the world. There are many people who lead a shut-in life, devoid of human contacts, and the only bright spot in their existence is the company of a toy

89

dog. Most toys are representatives of ancient breeds and their value as intimate associates has been recognized through the ages.

The members of this group are pets in every sense of the word and base their claim for attention on the comfort and satisfaction they give their owners. Among the specific breeds in this group are the Affenpinscher, Brussels Griffon, Chihuahua, Chinese Crested Dog, English Toy Spaniel, Italian Greyhound, Japanese Chin, Maltese, Manchester Terrier, Miniature Pinscher, Papillon, Pekingese, Pomeranian, Toy Poodle, Pug, Shih Tzu, Silky Terrier and Yorkshire Terrier.

The Chihuahua and Mexican Hairless originated in Mexico. Both breeds have many terrier traits. The Chihuahua is very active and quite popular, weighing from two to six pounds. The Mexican Hairless has become a rather rare breed. It is generally hairless, except for tufts of hair on its head and tail.

The English toy spaniels — a grouping of the Prince Charles, King Charles, Ruby and Blenheim spaniels into one class — vary from nine to 12 pounds. They really are miniature spaniels, beautiful and gentle, and make truly fine pets.

The origin of the Brussels Griffon is obvious. Originally a street urchin, the Brussels Griffon won the favor of the royal Belgian court in the late 1800s. Queen Henrietta Marie took great interest in the little dogs. The dog comes in small and medium sizes, docked and cropped and rough coated. A smooth-coated variety is known as *Petit Brabancon*.

An Italian Greyhound is a miniature of the English Greyhound, weighing between six and 10 pounds. The breed is believed to have originated in the Mediterranean basin more than 2000 years ago. It has been a favorite of royalty, including Anne of Denmark, Catherine the Great and Queen Victoria, who liked

Below: A King Charles Cavalier Spaniel.
Opposite: The Brussels Griffon is a cross between the German Affenpinscher and the Belgian Chien Barbe.

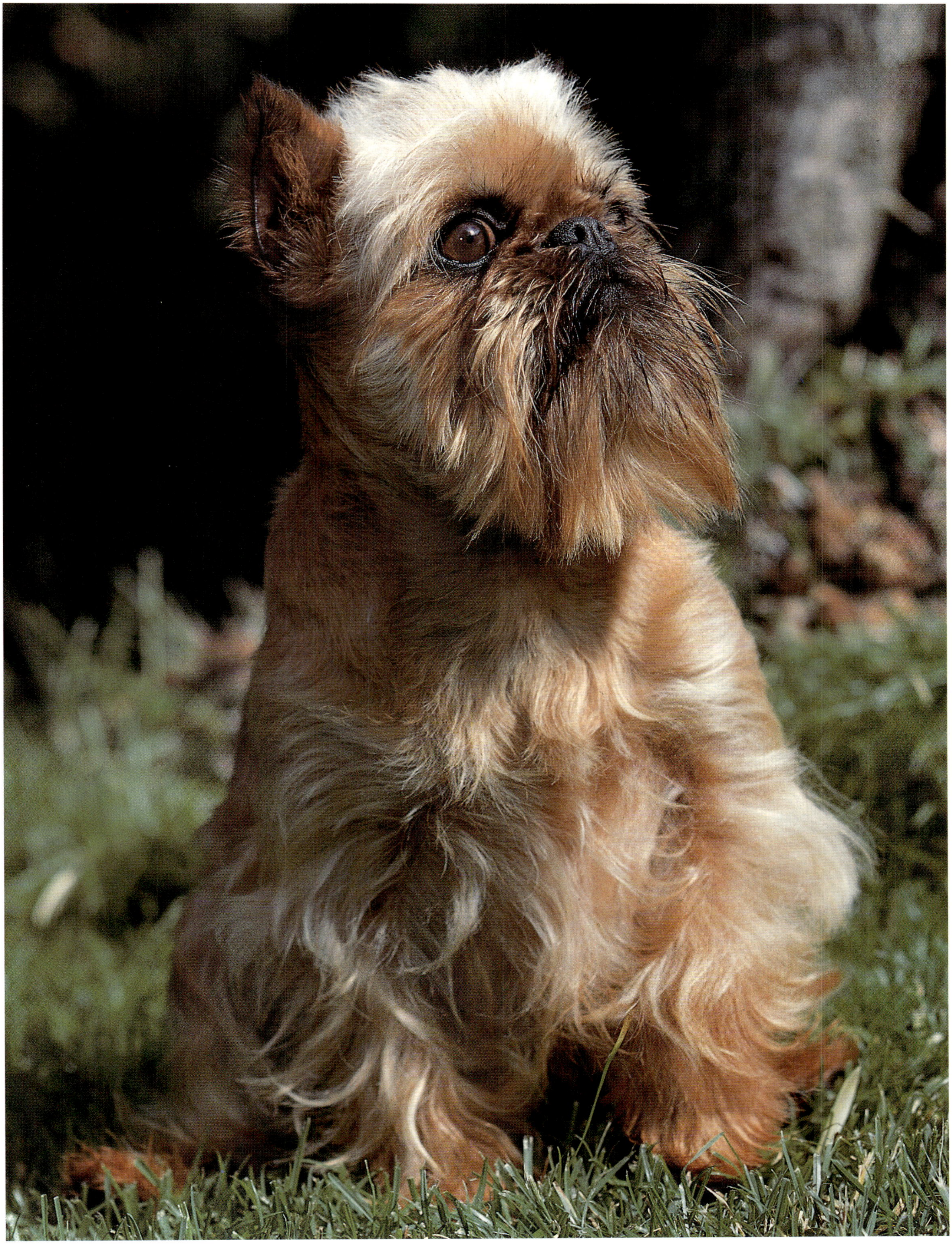

Below: The tiny Japanese Chin.
Bottom: A pair of Maltese puppies.
Opposite: The Greyhound, Whippet and Italian Greyhound are elegant animals bred for racing.

them so well that she bred them in her kennels. The Italian Greyhound, like its larger cousin, can catch rabbits on the run, reaching speeds up to 40 miles per hour. While it may have begun as a hunting dog, today the little Greyhound is an affectionate house pet, happy to snuggle by the fire and sleep with its owner.

The Japanese Chin weighs between four and nine pounds and is an active, interesting little fellow. It has long, somewhat silky hair and is either black and white or red and white. It is a beautiful little dog, the favorite of Japanese emperors for more than a 1000 years. The required white streak between their wide set eyes gives the breed a quizzical look and adds to their beauty.

Maltese dogs are alert and fearless and should weigh less than seven pounds — under

93

Below: The Pekingese, bred in the court of the Chinese emperors, was introduced to the West during the nineteenth century.
Opposite: The Papillon has an abundant, flowing coat.

three pounds is considered ideal. The long, white, silky coat reaches the ground and gives a striking appearance. The Maltese is another ancient breed.

The Papillon is an interesting little chap, weighing under nine pounds. The large, upright ears give the impression of butterfly wings and it is often called 'the butterfly dog.'

The Pekingese, or 'Peke,' is the aristocratic little lion dog from ancient China. It is probably the most popular member in the toy group and deserves this ranking because of its courage and personality. If a little dog may be said to be imposing, then the term applies to the Peke. It can weigh as much as 14 pounds. The smaller ones, or 'sleeve Pekes,' are thought to be the most desirable. Pekes love to romp about and are very active dogs.

The Pomeranian runs a close second to the Peke in popularity, and is a vivacious, intelligent animal. Its snappy gait attracts attention as it prances along on the leash. It is a beautiful dog in coat, coloring and proportion, with a striking resemblance to the

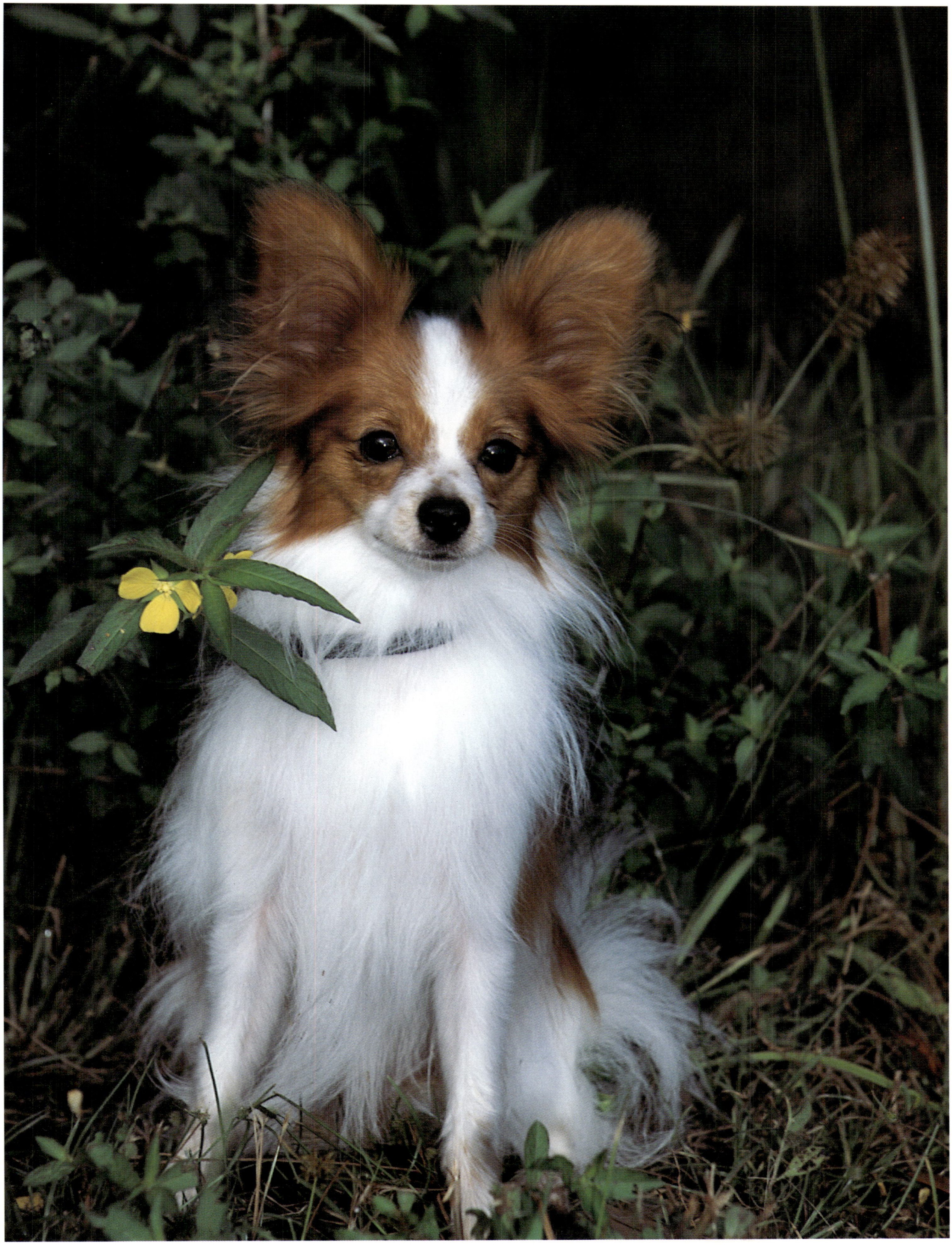

Clockwise from below: A portfolio of puppies, two Chinese Cresteds, a Shih Tzu, and a Pug.

Samoyed. It generally weighs under five pounds.

The Pug originally came from China and was a favorite of Tibetan monks. Dutch traders brought the Pug to Europe. It has enjoyed great popularity through the centuries, even being adopted as a mascot by the Dutch House of Orange. It is a gentle, lovable dog, weighing from 14 to 18 pounds. The Pug was, at one time, the real favorite of the toy group. Like any pet, the Pug has its flaws, such as snoring. Still, it is a wonderful companion dog. Its impish and charming personality more than makes up for its wrinkled face and serious expression.

One of the most unusual dogs believed to have originated in China is the Chinese Crested. This tiny dog is normally nearly hairless, though in nearly every litter there are 'powder puffs,' or puppies with hair. The Chinese Crested was nearly extinct in 1966, with the only known specimens belonging to an elderly American. Today the tiny, fine boned dog with a silky topknot and hairy feet and tail is a well established breed.

Toy Black-and-Tan Terriers are really small Manchester terriers weighing about

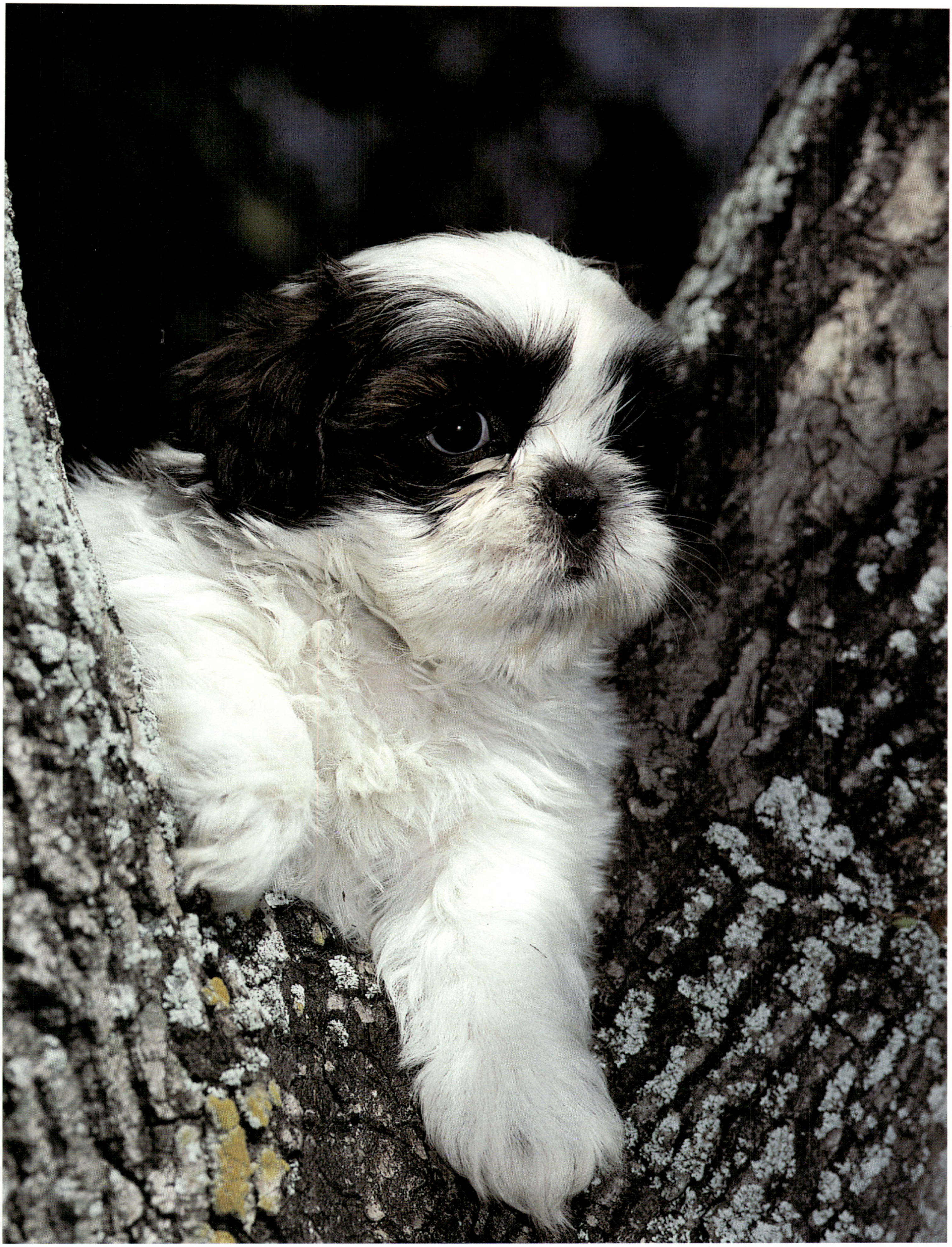

seven pounds. Developed in England as ratters, they are very active and intelligent.

Toy Poodles are bright little fellows, weighing less than 12 pounds. They may be any solid color.

Miniature Pinschers resemble the Doberman, but weigh only six to 10 pounds. Like the Doberman Pinscher, the breed originated in Germany. They were named 'Reh Pinscher' because of their similarities to a very small species of deer. Very active and bright, they were once listed as a part of the Terrier group.

The silky coat of a dark, steel-blue color gives the Yorkshire Terrier its outstanding appearance. 'Yorkies,' in spite of their long mantle of hair reaching to the ground, have the sporting instincts of larger terriers. Originally, they were working dogs, bred by English weavers to fit into a pocket. Yet they are bold enough to kill rats. Weighing only four to seven pounds, the Yorkshire Terrier eventually became a popular lap dog. Despite their small size, Yorkies are good watchdogs, easily trained to bark at a knock on the door. They like both children and cats.

Below right: The Miniature Pinscher bears a strong resemblance to the Doberman except in size.
Bottom: An irresistible pack of Toy Poodle puppies.
Opposite: The Yorkshire Terrier, known affectionately as the 'Yorkie,' is a popular pet.
Overleaf: A pair of Yorkies.

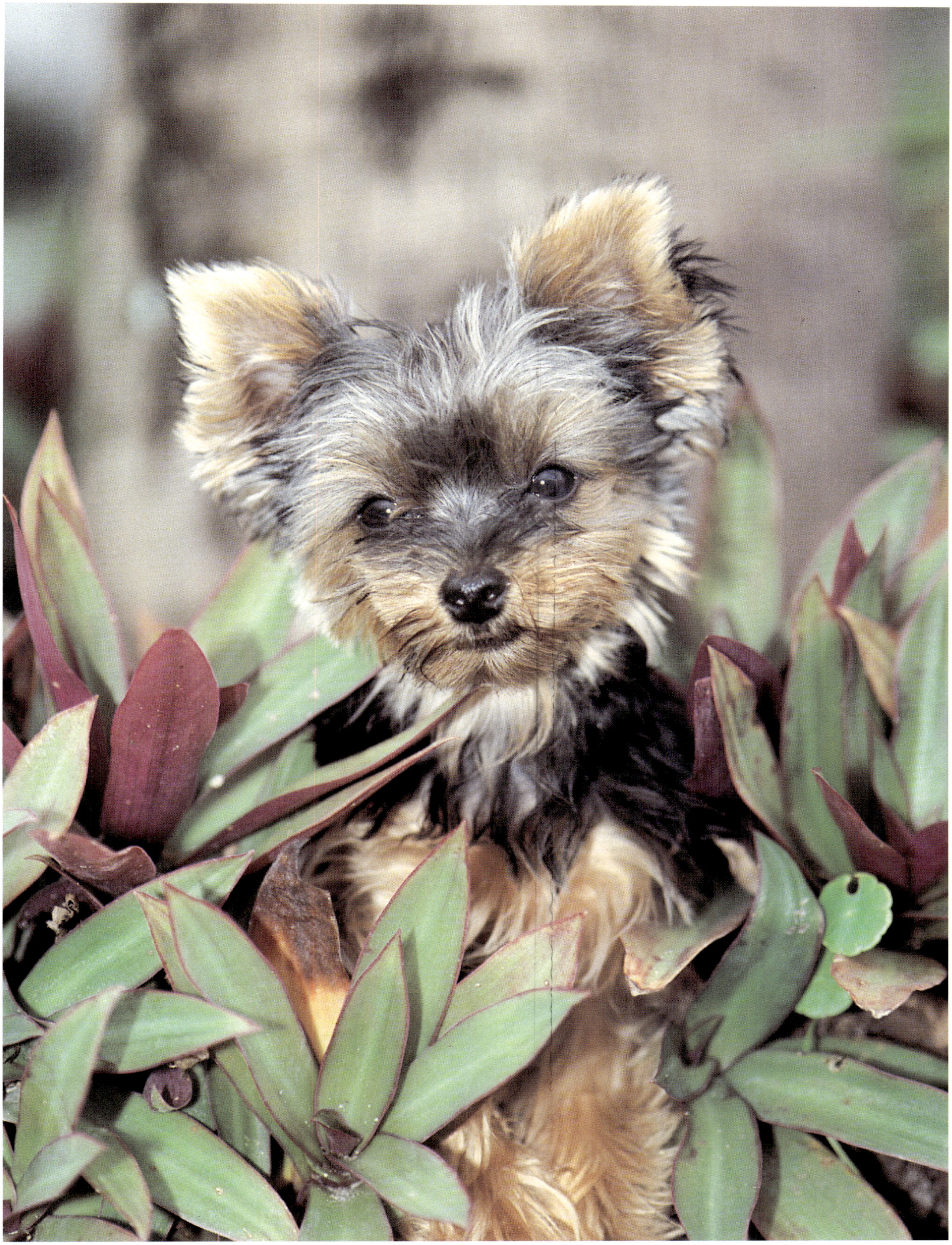

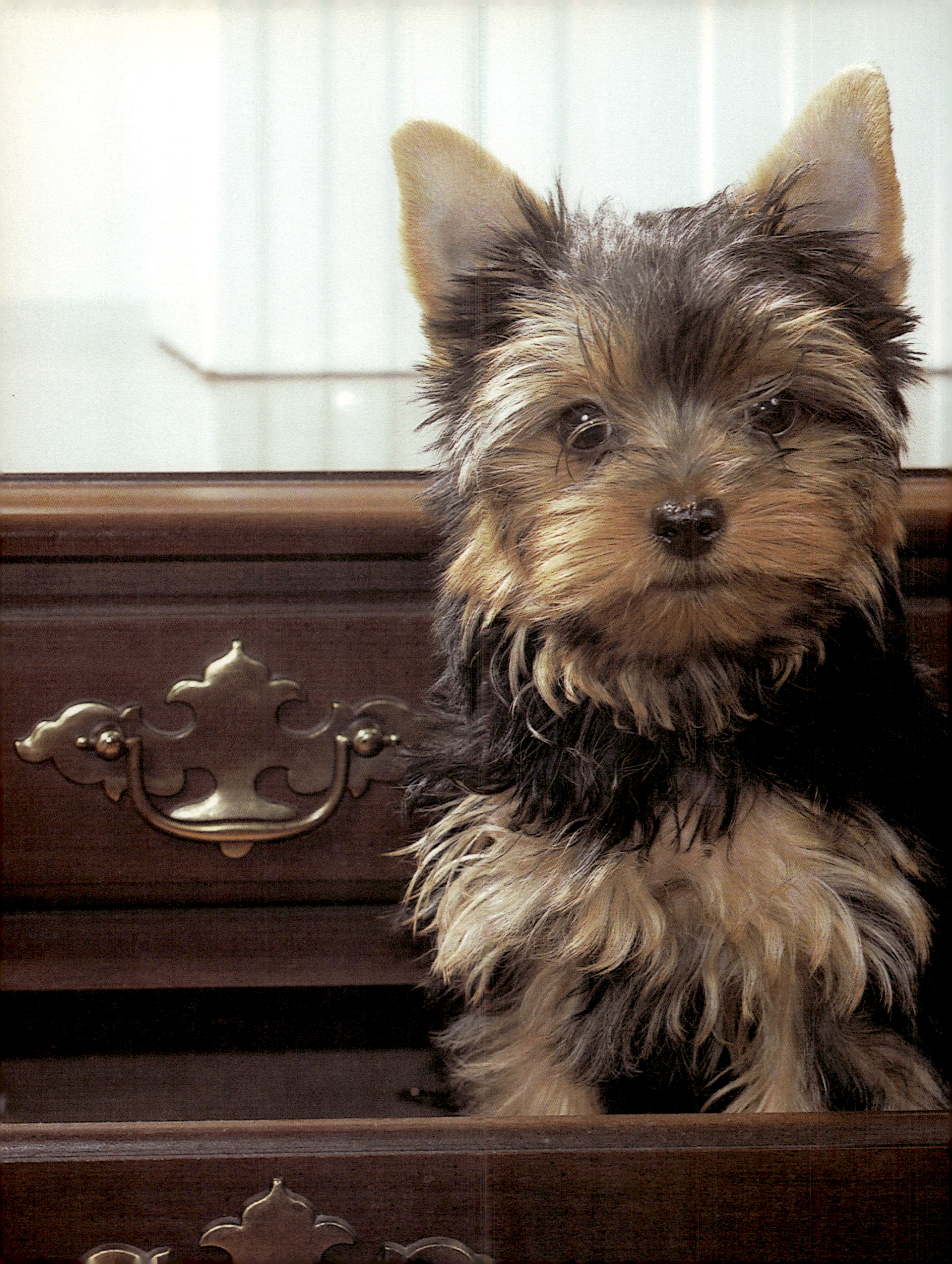

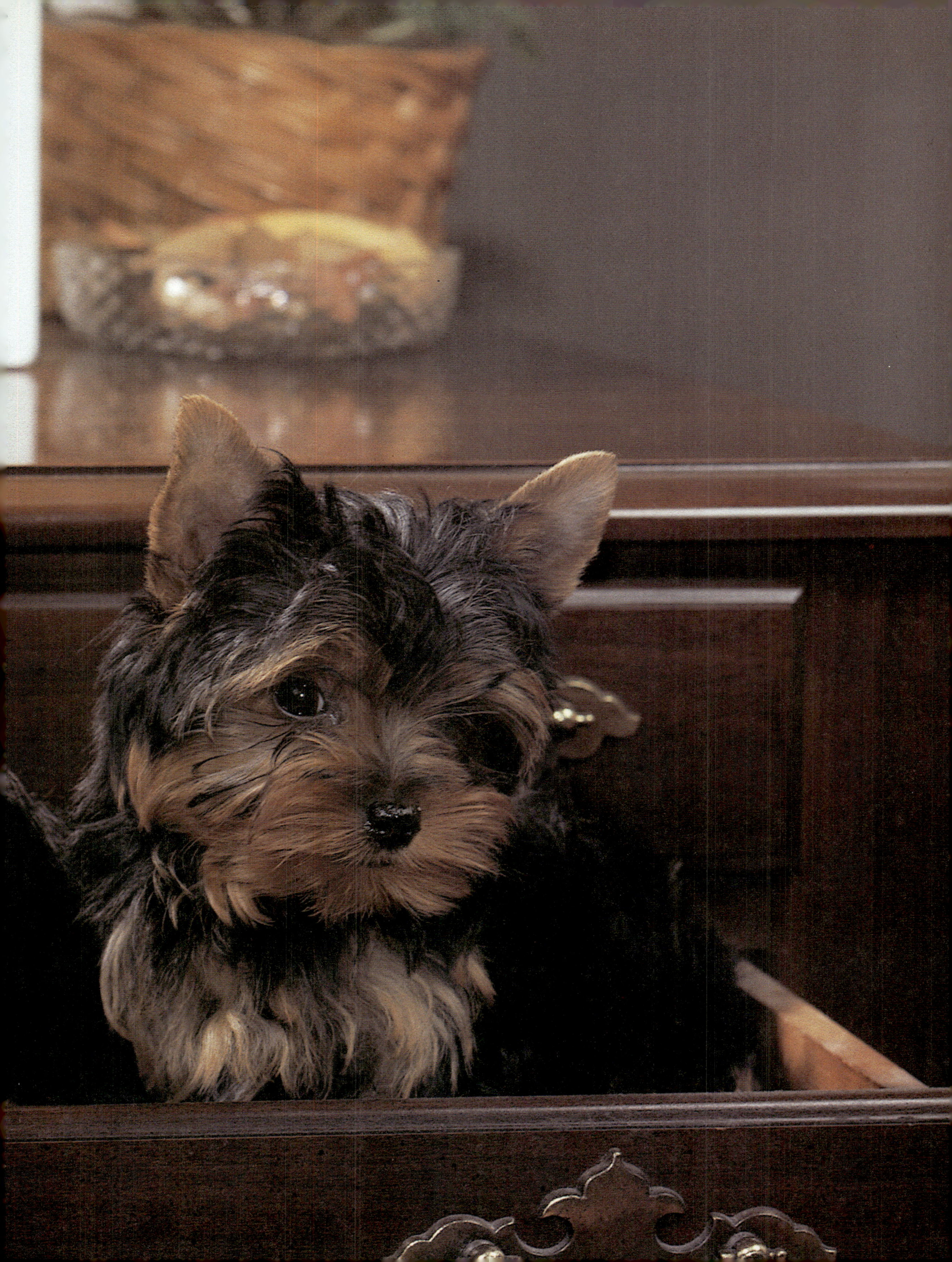

SPORTING DOGS

Below: One of today's most popular canines is the Labrador Retriever.
Opposite: The Labrador Retriever was originally bred as a hunting dog.

Sporting dogs are those which were traditionally used as retrievers by hunters. These include, but are not limited to, typed such as the setters, the spaniels, the pointers and, of course, the retrievers.

Among the many breeds of sporting dogs are: Pointer, German Shorthaired Pointer, German Wirehaired Pointer, Chesapeake Bay Retriever, Curly-coated Retriever, Flat-coated Retriever, Golden Retriever, Labrador Retriever (Yellow, Chocolate and Black), English Setter, Irish Setter, Gordon Setter, American Water Spaniel, Brittany Spaniel, Clumber Spaniel, American Cocker Spaniel, English Cocker Spaniel, English Springer Spaniel, Field Spaniel, Irish Water Spaniel, Sussex Spaniel, Welsh Springer Spaniel, Vizsla, Weimaraner and Wirehaired Pointing Griffon.

The Chesapeake Bay Retrievers, Water Spaniels and retrievers were traditionally used for bringing in waterfowl, although some retrievers are effective for upland game. The Labrador Retriever is one of the most popular breeds anywhere. The 'Lab' is well known for its retrieving ability, good temperament, intelligence, amiability and

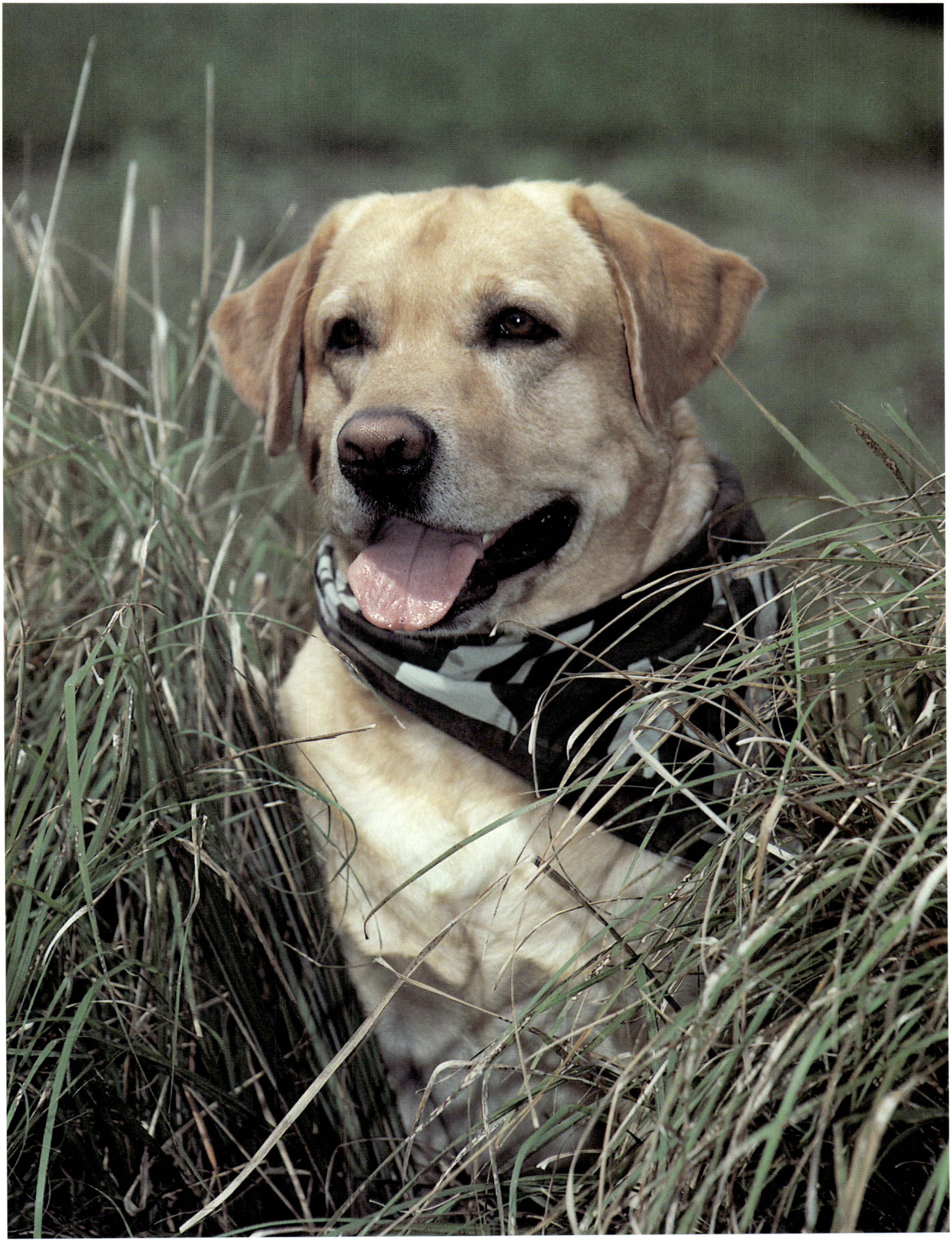

loyalty. They are excellent family dogs and will protect 'their' children to the death if necessary.

Labs were originally brought to England from Newfoundland (not Labrador), where they were popularized by the Earl of Malmsbury. In Britain, they were trained to flush and retrieve game, but have since been trained in many other fields. Labrador Retrievers have been used to sniff out mines in minefields, to locate illegal drugs, as guard dogs and as guide dogs for the blind. Though typically thought of as black, they also exist in yellow and chocolate brown.

The Golden Retriever is another of the world's most popular dogs. Like the Labrador Retriever, it is known for its hunting abilities and amiable temperament.

Below: The strong, handsome face of a loyal Labrador Retriever.
Opposite: The Golden Retriever is not only one of the most beautiful of dogs, but also one of the most intelligent.

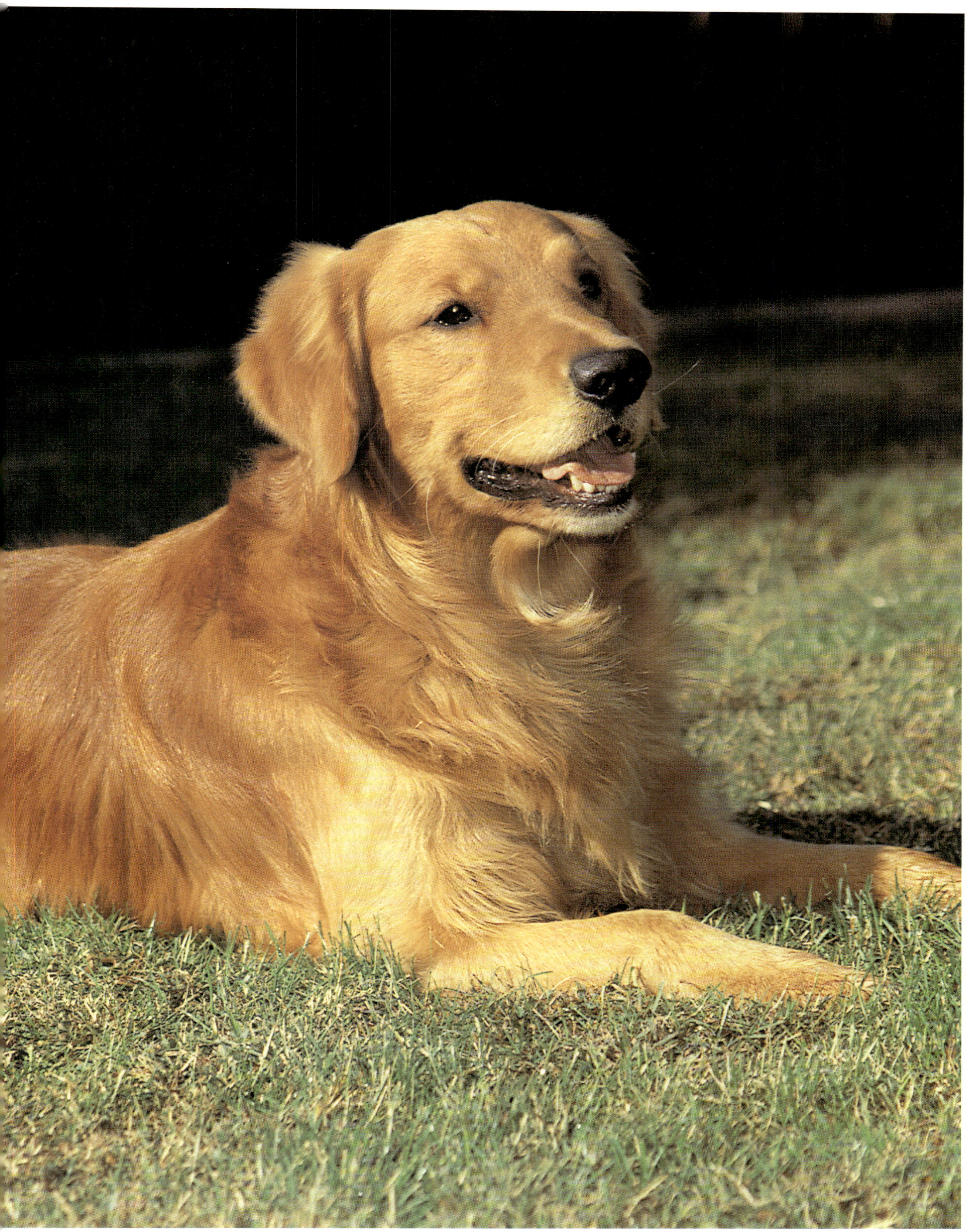

Below: The Irish Setter, originally bred to hunt, is an energetic and easy-tempered animal.
Opposite: First bred in England, the Golden Retriever is now a very popular breed on both sides of the Atlantic.

Highly intelligent, this breed has also been used as a guide dog for the blind. This breed is so sensitive to its owner's needs that one Golden Retriever is said to predict its owner's impending epileptic seizures. Oprah Winfrey, the famous talk show host, once said, 'Little dogs don't work for me. I have eight dogs, and all of them are big ones — Golden Retrievers and mixed breeds — because I'm an all-American, big-boned woman.'

The Golden Retriever originated in England in the early nineteenth century, bred by Sir Dudley Marjoribanks. At that time, hunting game birds like ducks and pheasants was extremely popular. Sir Dudley wanted to breed a dog that could retrieve downed birds from icy waters. He was so successful that even today the Golden Retriever is known for its retrieving ability. Yet, this retriever is also a great family dog, protective of the children and eager to please its owner.

The pointers and setters (English, Irish, and Gordon) are used to find birds such as grouse, quail and pheasant, which they locate from body scents in the air. Their work is performed in a beautiful fashion, impressive to watch. They range wide and freeze to a point when the game is located. Hunting ability is instinctive, but a certain amount of training is desirable to bring the animal to perfection.

The pointers were the first dogs to stand and point game. Neat and trim, they are graceful and active in the field. Even the untrained pointer, raised as a pet or family dog, will point instinctively at birds and game. The poise shown by a well bred pointer or

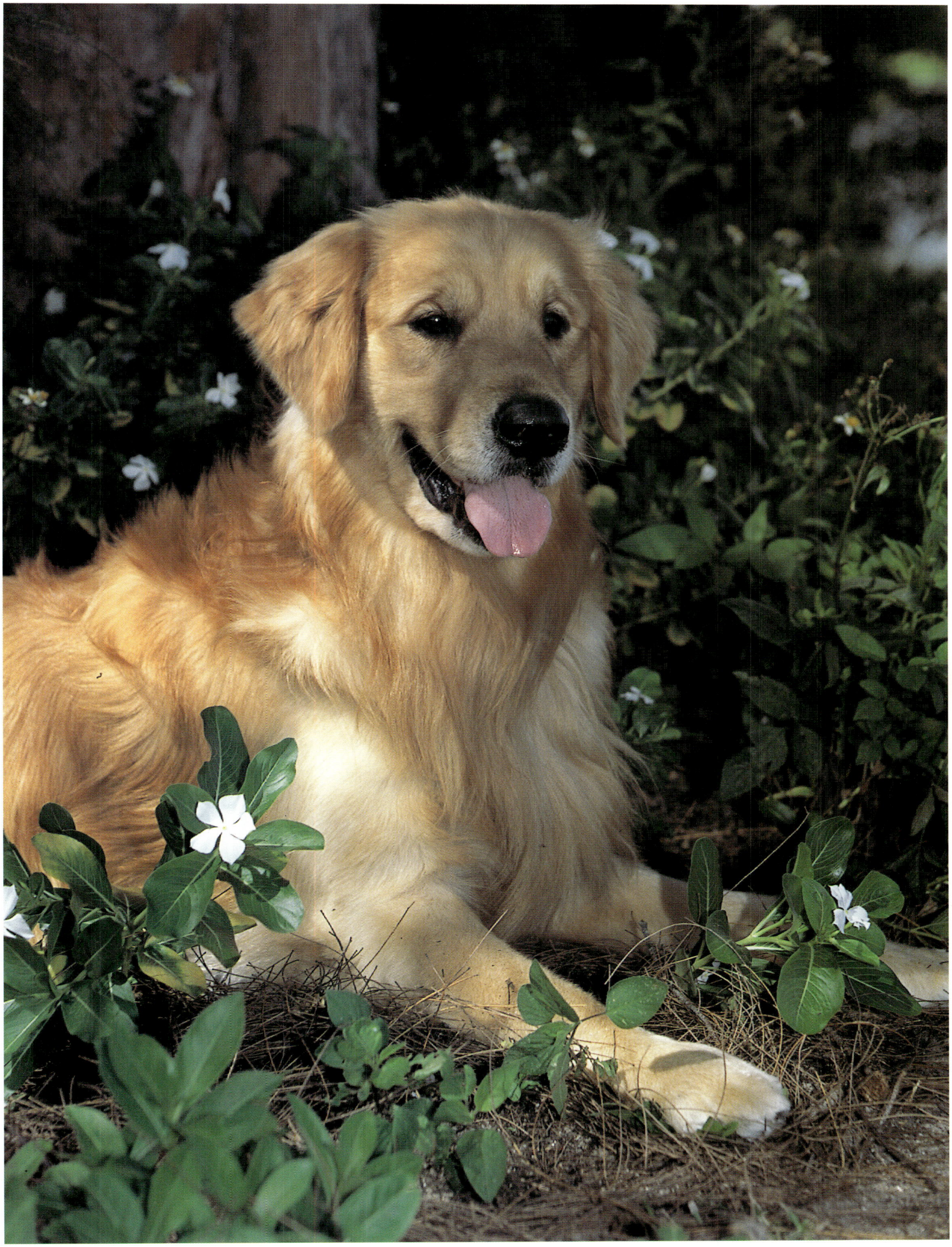

Below: A good profile view of an American Cocker Spaniel.
Opposite: A Cocker Spaniel puppy. The breed is a popular pet and good with children.

setter when in action is a wonderful sight. Many of the dogs will retrieve the birds after they have been shot. The Wirehaired Pointing Griffon works in a fashion similar to that of a pointer and, protected by its shaggy coat, is especially good in rough country.

The English Setter was created from a cross between the Spanish Pointer and the Land Spaniel. The two men who had the most influence upon the breed were Edward Laverack and Purcell Llewellyn. In fact, many people believe that there is a particular breed called the Llewellyn Setter. These dogs are actually English Setters, bred by Llewellyn at his kennel.

Spaniels originated in Spain as the name implies, but variations on the breed have been developed many places, especially in England and North America. The Cocker Spaniel is perhaps the most popular of all the spaniels. The American Cocker, the smallest dog in the sporting group, was developed in the United States from the English Cocker Spaniel. The American Cocker is much smaller than its English counterpart, and also has a thicker, longer coat and a more cleanly chiseled head with a shorter muzzle. While the American Cocker is popular in the United States, the English Cocker is far more popular worldwide.

The spaniels, who work with their eyes and nose to the ground, are good for birds and other small game. They are particularly well suited for country environments, where

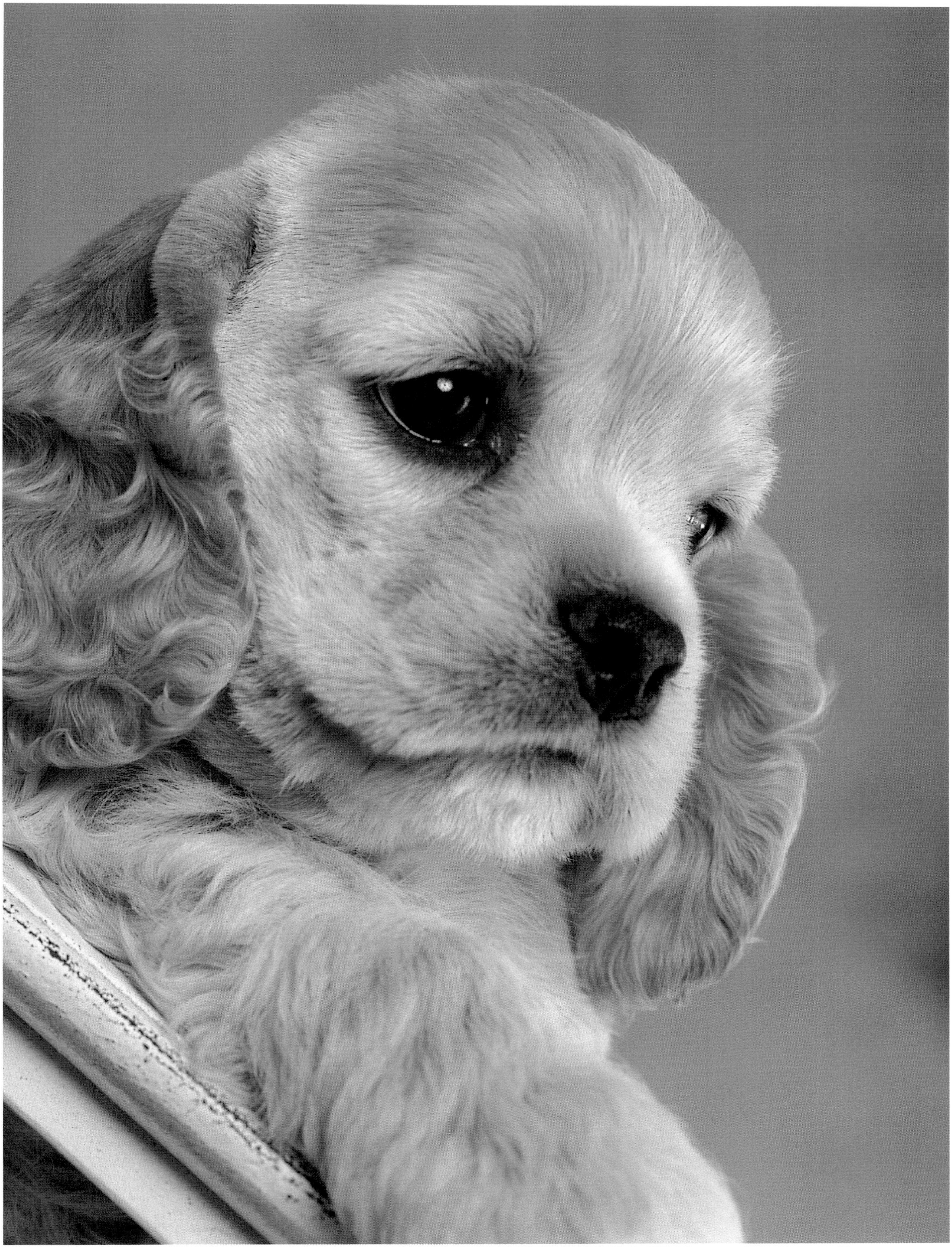

Below: Named for the German city-state of Weimar, in whose court they were originally bred, Weimaraners are popular hunting dogs.
Opposite: An English Cocker Spaniel.
Overleaf: First cousin to the English Cocker is the English Springer Spaniel.

larger bird dogs cannot easily hunt. Being low to the ground, spaniels can negotiate dense cover. When close to the quarry, the spaniel's tail moves quickly, except for the Brittany Spaniel, which points to its game. The larger ones, such as the Clumber Spaniel, work more slowly than their smaller brothers. All spaniels will retrieve on either land or water, with the larger ones having an advantage in the latter element. The interest shown in field trials for spaniels indicate a healthy regard for this group. Field trials for any sporting dogs give an idea of an animal's performance under working conditions and should be considered in addition to their bench show record. All weights and sizes given below are for male dogs, which are somewhat taller and heavier than the females of the same breed.

Chesapeake Bay Retrievers weigh from 60 to 75 pounds and measure 23 to 26 inches at the shoulders. The other retrievers, while about the same weight, are generally somewhat shorter. English Setters weigh from 40 to 45 pounds and are about 22 inches in height. The Pointer and other setters vary somewhat from this weight and size. The Clumber Spaniel is the heaviest of the spaniels, weighing as much as 65 pounds in some cases; the Springer, about 45 pounds; and the Cocker, the smallest, between 18 and 24 pounds.

No dogs in this group have cropped ears and all have weather resistant coats, with the exception of the Pointer. The dogs in this sporting group find and retrieve the game, but the hunter must kill it. The history of sporting dogs, particularly in early times, is probably more complete than that of almost any other group, as these dogs were used by the wealthier class. Early authors, especially the English, devoted much time and effort to give accurate descriptions of hunting breeds and hunting conditions.

Since the dogs were bred and used for hunting and sporting purposes, it necessarily follows that they have been wonderful companions under most conditions. The outstanding characteristics of the group are a gentle nature and lovable disposition. Their devotion, dependability and quiet manner make them ideal pets and companions. They are reserved or spirited as the occasion, or the owner's mood, dictates. Members of this group are used in many instances as pets only, and the great popularity of the spaniels, particularly the Cocker and English Cocker spaniels, is a tribute to their adaptability as an all-round dog.

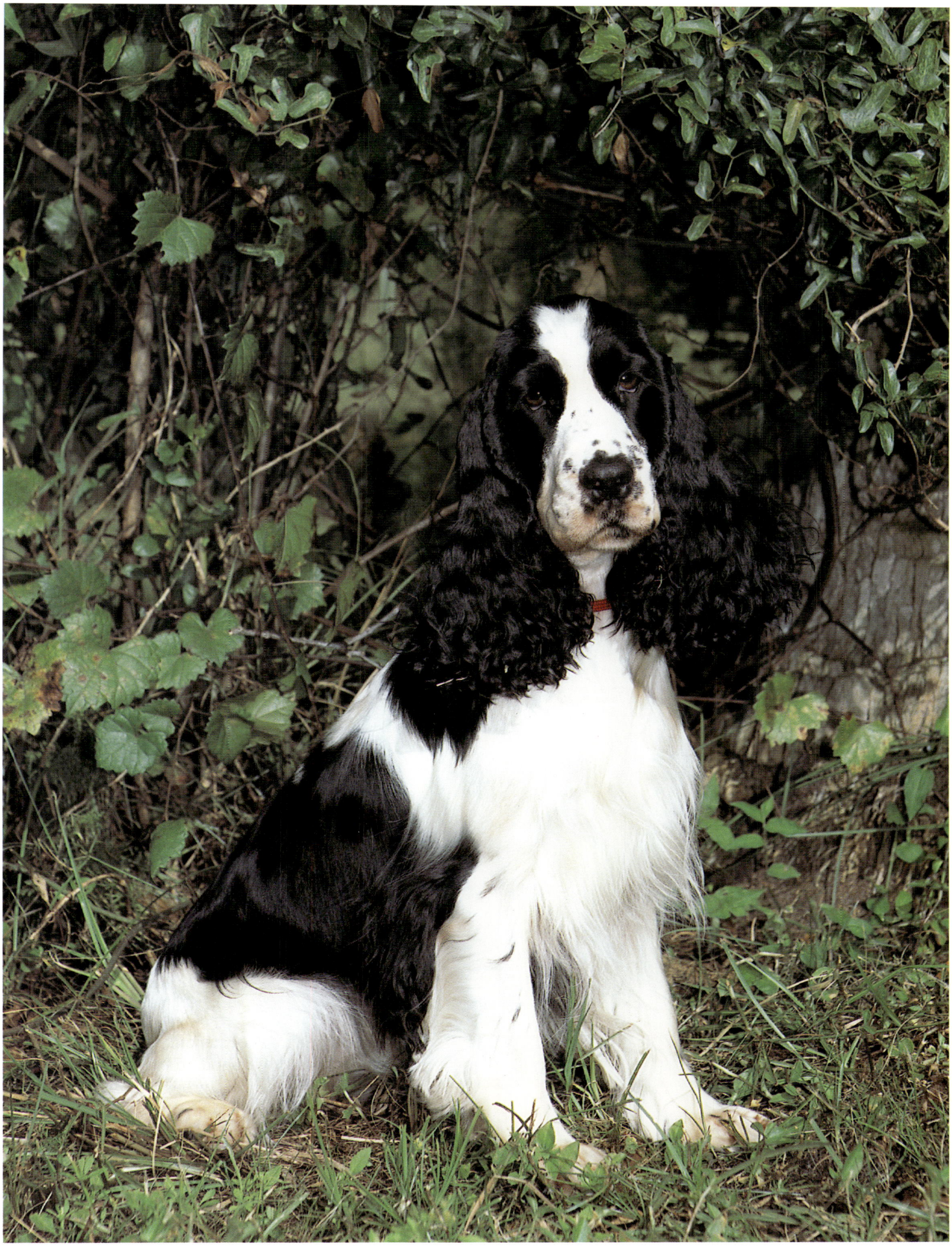

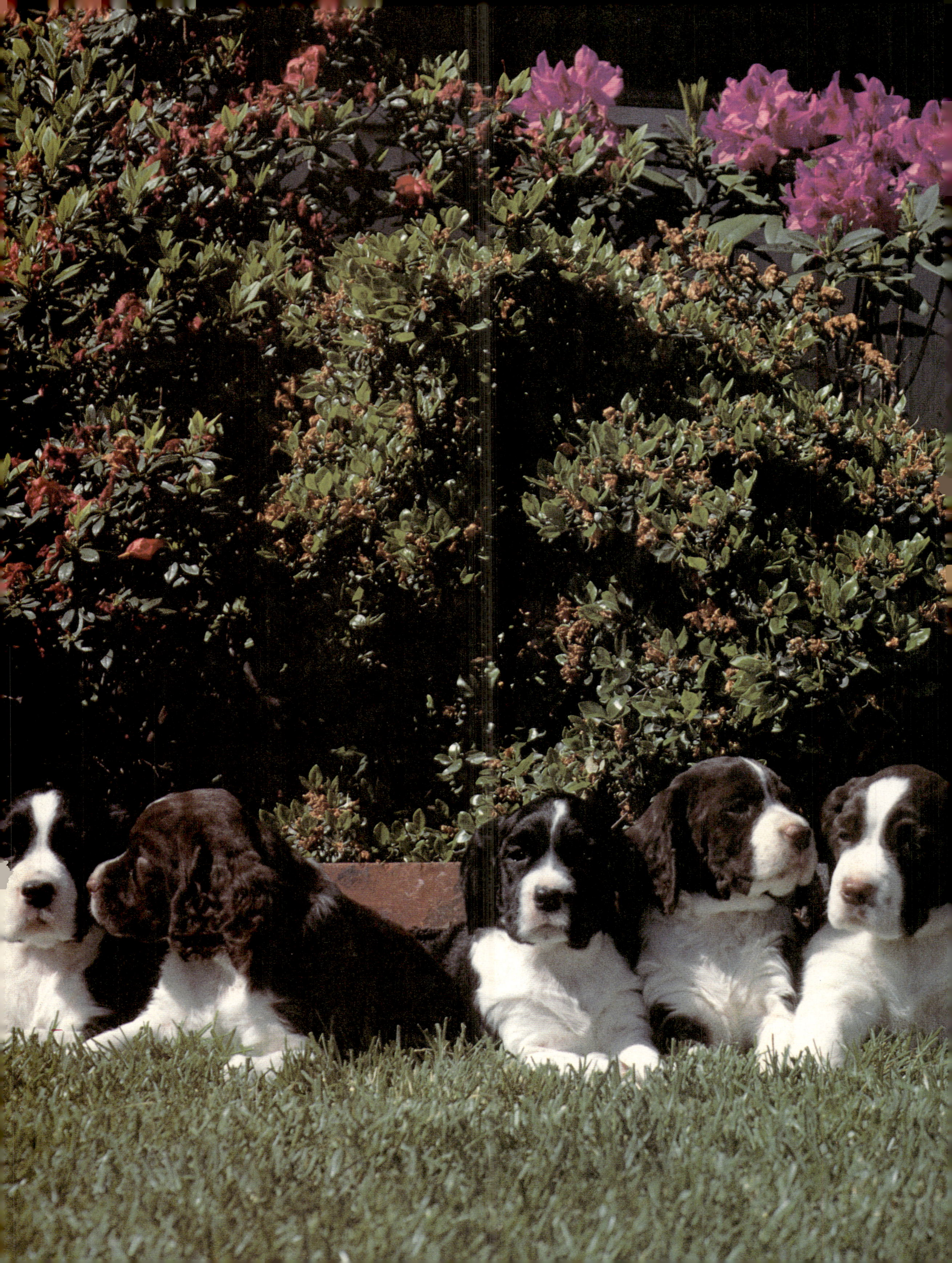

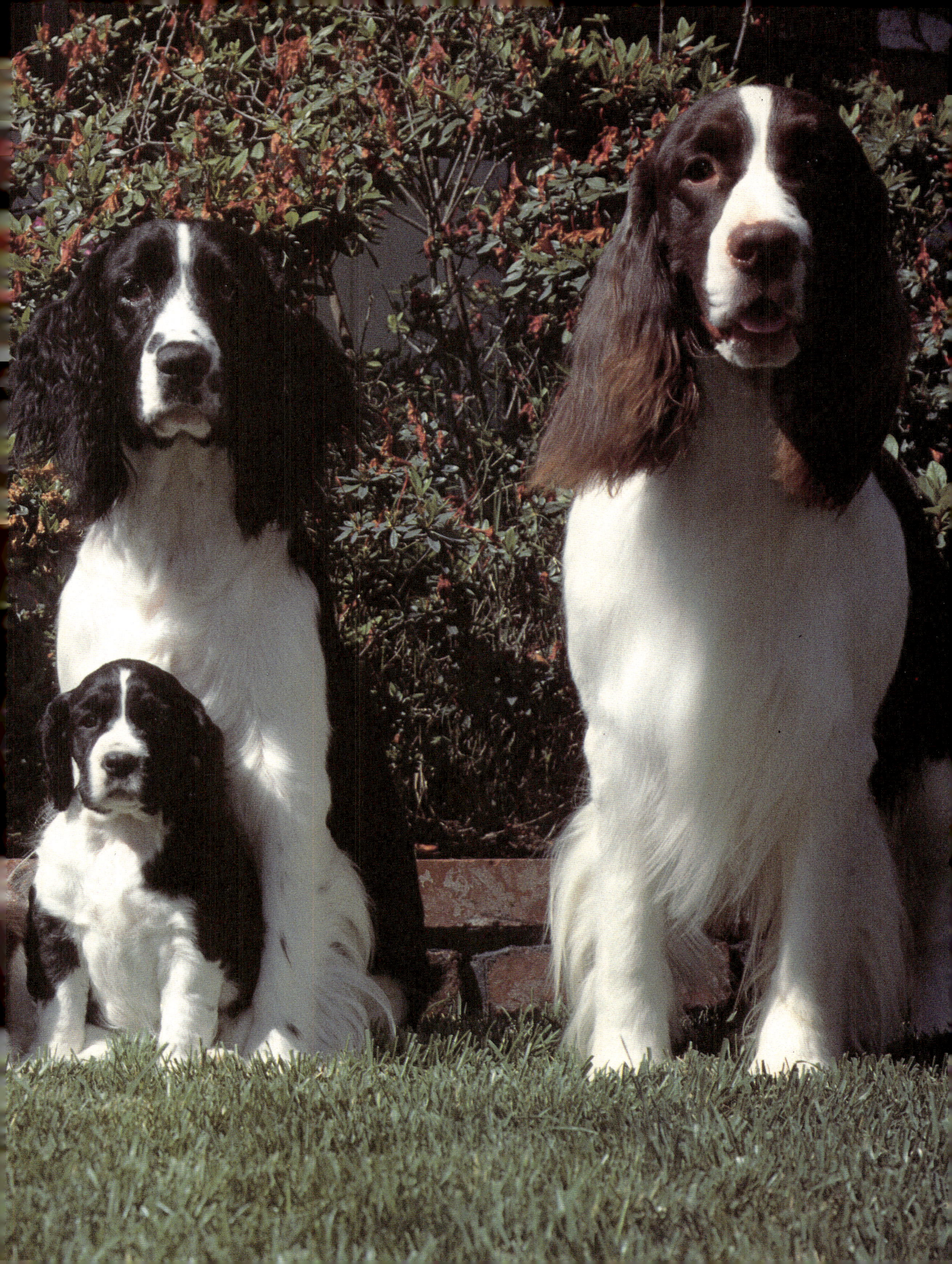

NON-SPORTING BREEDS

Below: A Standard Poodle, clipped in the traditional fashion.
Opposite: A Poodle puppy.

The non-sporting dogs are those which are bred almost entirely as pets, companions or show dogs. Some such breeds, such as the Poodle, were once hunting dogs, but are now primarily show and companion dogs, no longer considered a member of the sporting breeds. Indeed, the Dalmatian, like the Standard Poodle, retains latent sporting instincts which may be emphasized at some future time.

Among the breeds of this type are the Bichon Frisé, Boston Terrier, Bulldog, Chow Chow, Dalmatian, Finnish Spitz, French Bulldog, Keeshond, Lhasa Apso, Miniature Poodle, Standard Poodle, Schipperke, Shar-Pei, Tibetan Spaniel and Tibetan Terrier.

The Standard Poodle was originally developed in Germany as a water retriever. Like other retrievers, Poodles are easily trained and their abilities make them great

115

Below and opposite: The Boston Terrier was one of the first breeds to be developed in the United States. They are popular as show dogs, or simply as loyal pets.

all-round dogs. In Russia, large and usually black Poodles were used to pull milk carts. They became so popular in France, they were chosen to be the national dog. In fact, the Poodle is so closely associated with France that many people still call it the French Poodle. The Poodle is one of the favorite subjects of artists and probably appears in more paintings than any other breed of dog. Botticelli, Dürer, Rembrandt and Goya all included Poodles in their paintings. The Standard Poodle is considered to be an ideal choice for the active family.

Miniature Poodles are small editions of the Standard Poodles, weighing under 20 pounds and standing between 10 and 15 inches tall. Like their larger cousins, they are very active and require daily exercise.

The Boston Terrier is an American-bred dog. This breed is a perennial favorite — fashions change but the Boston's popularity remains the same. It is a clean-looking, short-coated, animated dog which adapts itself to any surroundings. Its black and white or brindle and white coloring make it look as if it is dressed in a tuxedo, ready for a formal

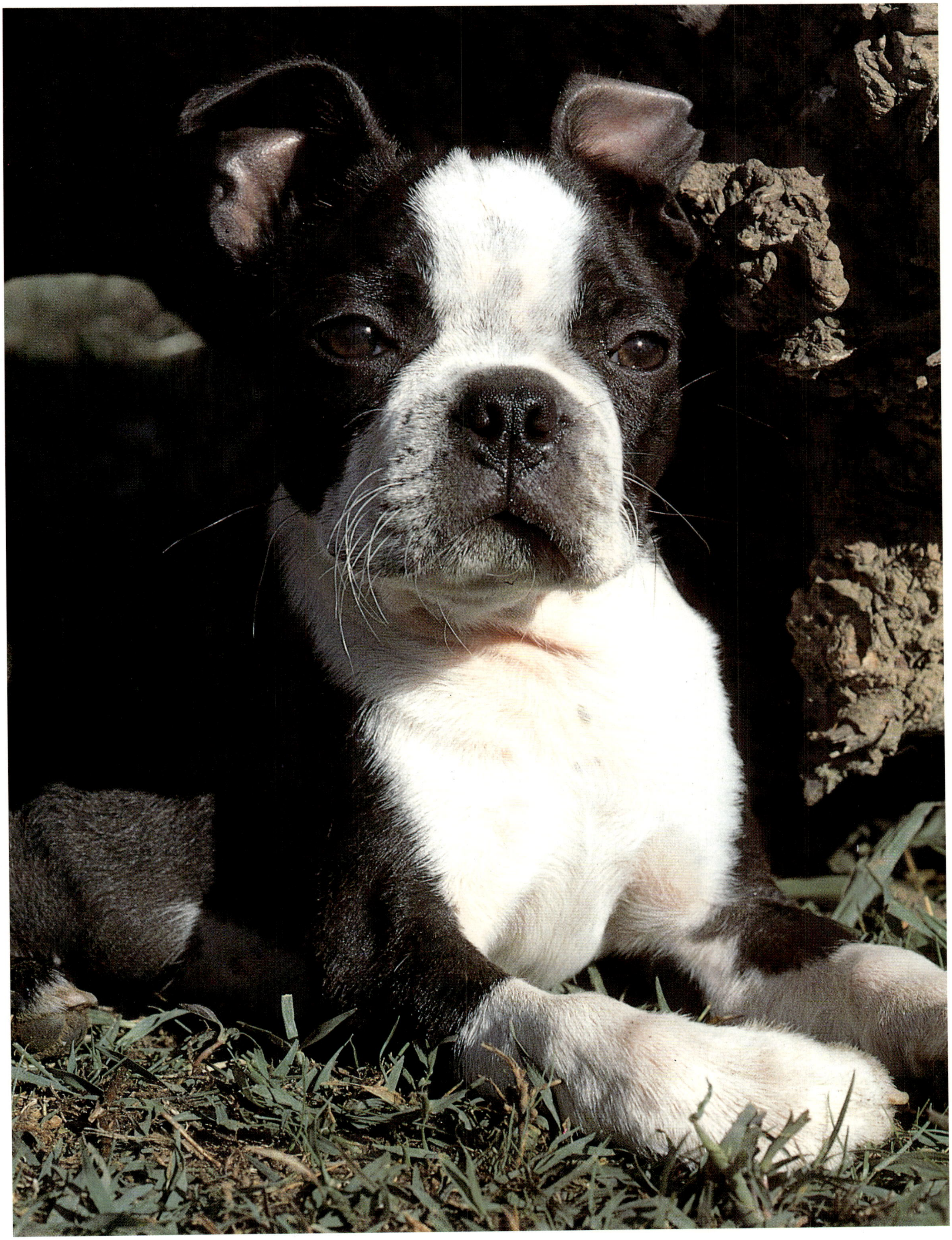

Below: The Chow Chow originated in China, where it is variously referred to as the 'bear dog' or the 'wolf dog,' although it looks like a lion.
Opposite top and bottom: The English Bulldog is a tenacious animal and much better tempered than it appears.

ball. Yet its playful manner makes it a popular companion dog.

Bulldogs are extremely gentle and thoroughly tractable, despite their somewhat pugnacious facial expressions and traditional purpose. Short coated and weighing about 50 pounds, the breed was used for bull baiting in England. Happily, that 'sport' has been abolished and the Bulldog is now a pet, companion and guardian. In this latter respect, the Bulldog may be relied on completely. The Bulldog is justifiably credited with being one of the most courageous of dogs, and an outstanding characteristic is its tenacity of purpose — once committed, the dog is there for keeps.

The French Bulldog, or *Bouledog Francais,* is a splendid, mild-mannered animal. They are descended from either the English Bulldog or a Spanish dog of the bulldog type. Weighing up to 28 pounds, they make good pets and guardians.

Chow Chows or just Chows, as they are generally known, are of Chinese origin and are truly beautiful animals. They are similar to the oldest fossilized dog — several million years old — found in America. The Chow was used in Asia as a hunting dog and to guard herds, sampans and junks. The largest Chows also pulled carts. The coat, mostly red or black, is quite abundant, with an ample ruff about the neck which accentuates their lionlike expression. A purebred Chow always has a distinct blue-black tongue.

The Chow is a short, powerfully built dog, compact and solid. Chows may have been more maligned than any other breed,

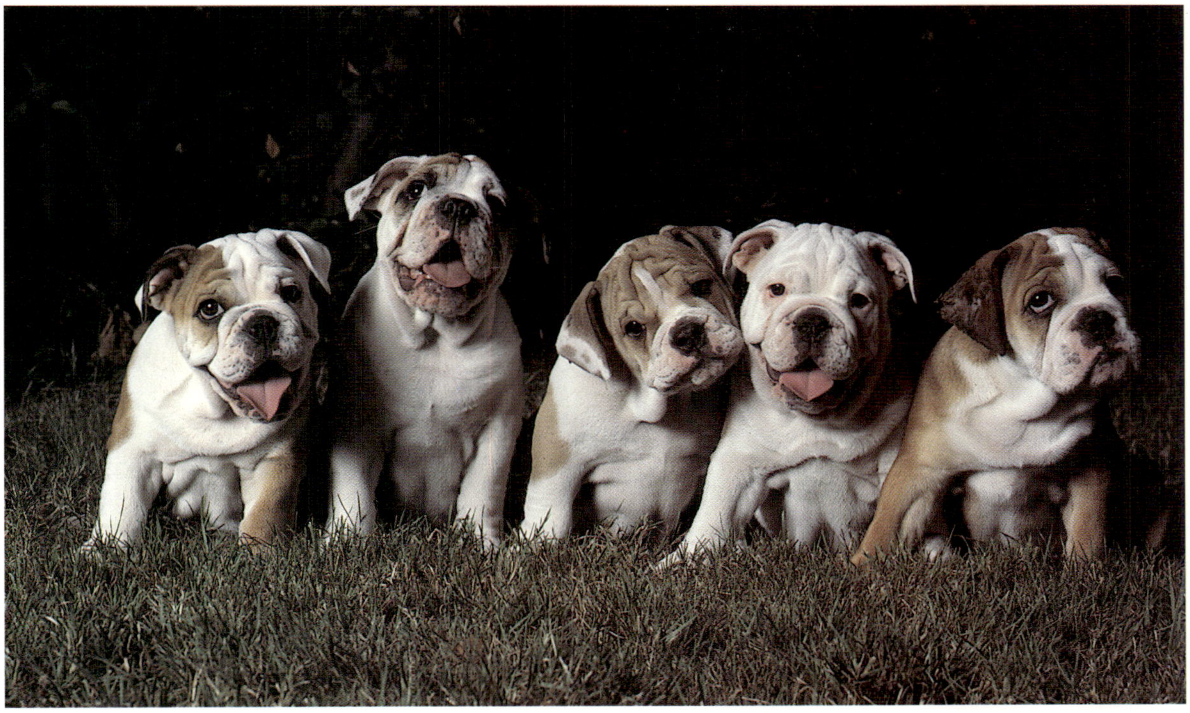

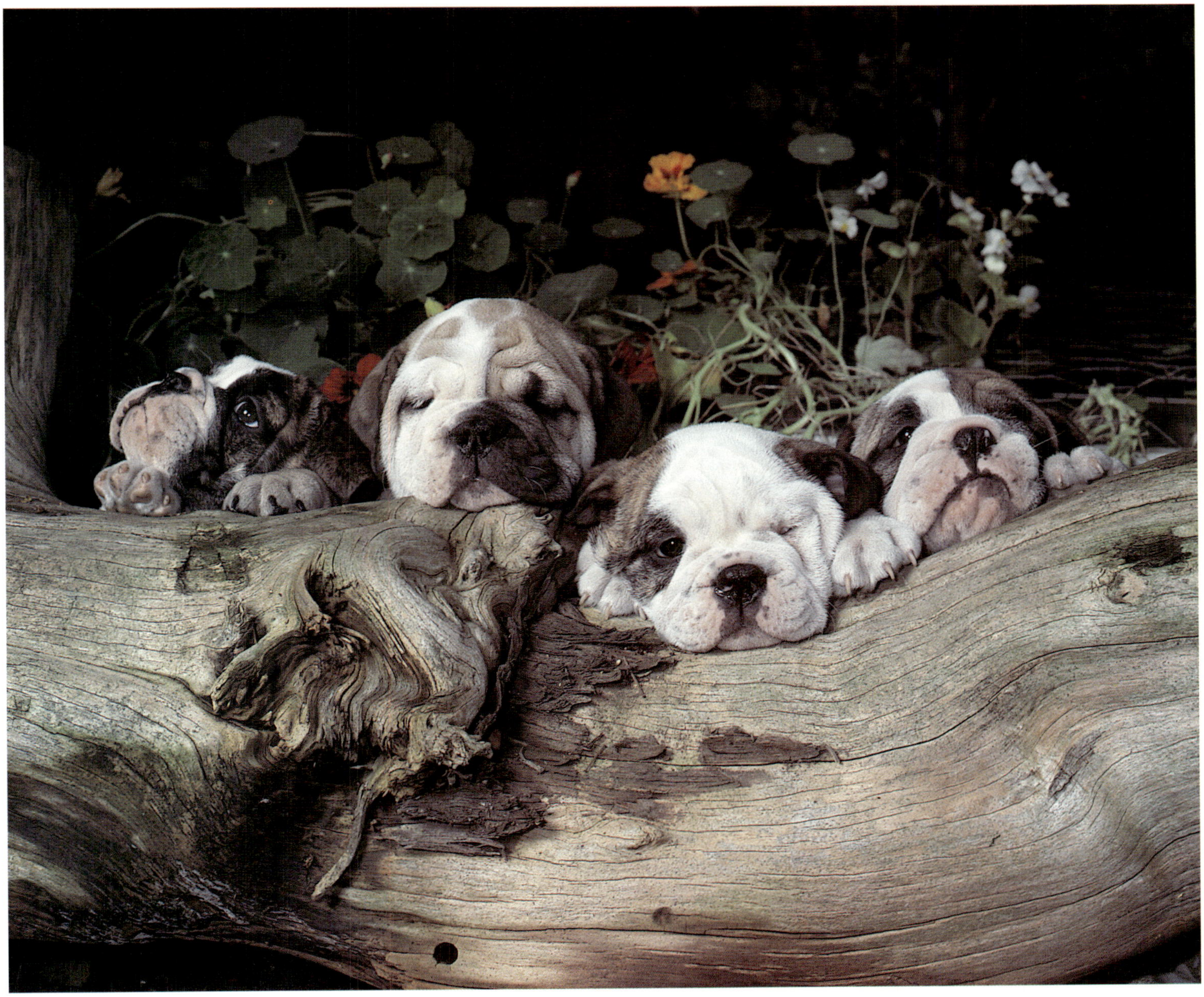

Right: Unmistakable in its appearance, the Dalmatian is a traditional favorite of fire-fighters.
Below and opposite: An increasingly popular show breed, the Shar-Pei has the amusing appearance of having a coat two sizes too large.

through lack of proper appreciation. They are canine individualists, refusing to be pushed into anything. They are intensely loyal to their owners and can be ferocious if provoked.

Like the Chow, the Shar-Pei is an ancient breed developed in China. It is believed that it is a relative of the Chow, since both breeds have purple tongues. By 1947 however, the Shar-Pei was nearly extinct, saved only by dedicated breeders in Hong Kong. The Shar-Pei was once a fighting dog, but today it is bred to be a family pet. Its loose skin and wrinkled face make it an unusual yet attractive dog. It has a very sweet and loving disposition.

The Dalmatian is the spotted dog invariably seen in every firehouse in the days of horse-drawn apparatus, and still known as 'the fire house dog.' The breed takes its name from Dalmatia, the coastal region overlooking the Adriatic Sea, of what is now

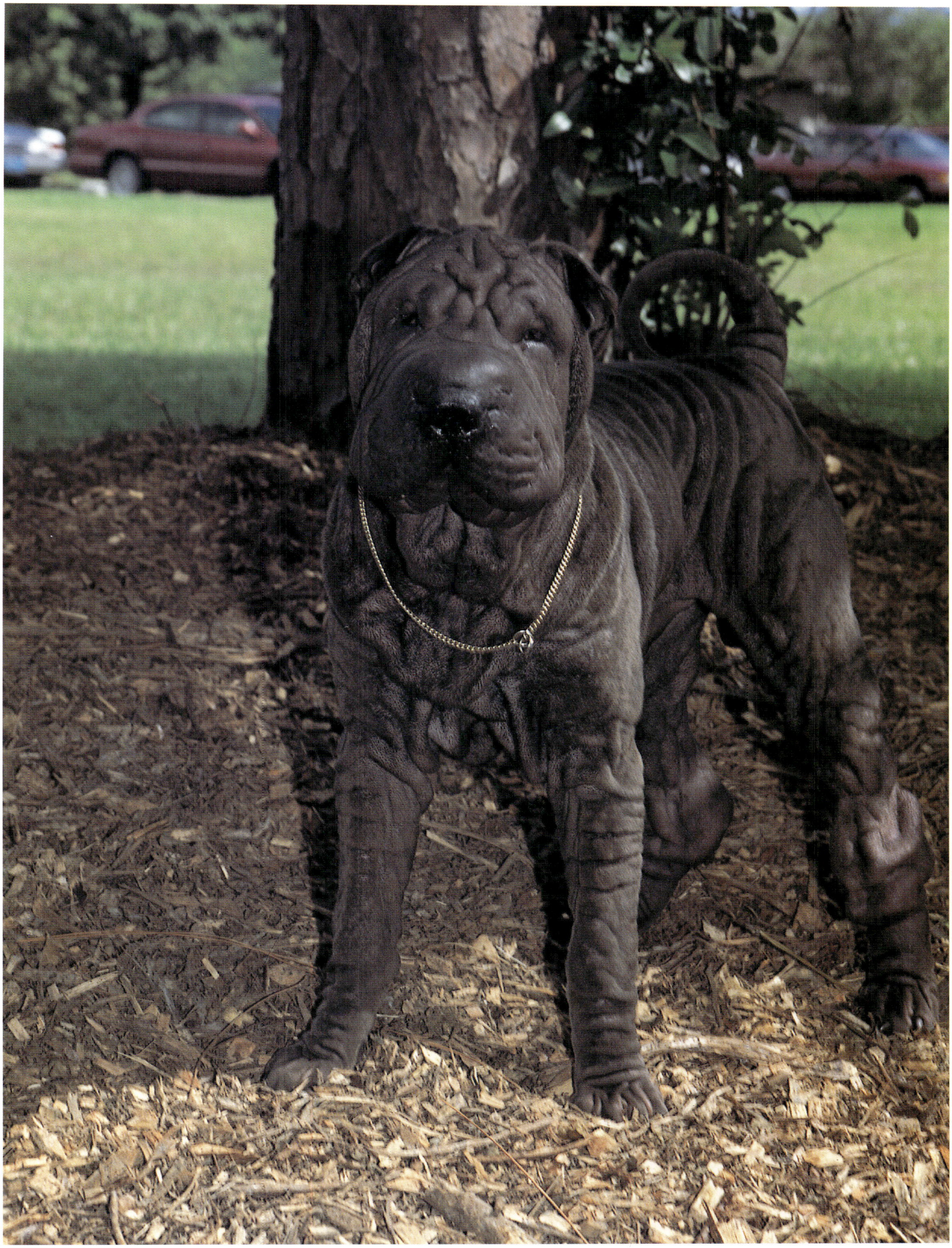

Below: The Dalmatian is actually born white, with the strikingly characteristic spots developing within the pup's first several weeks.

Opposite: The Schipperke, or 'Little Captain,' is an alert and lively dog.

Croatia. However, dogs resembling the Dalmatian have been depicted in paintings and frescoes in Egypt and Greece. Countries that claim the breed range from Denmark to India. While still common in Croatia and the former Yugoslavian region, the Dalmatian began as a working dog, serving as a messenger in wartime. It is also now used as a bird dog, a guard dog and even as a sled dog. Weighing up to 50 pounds, the Dalmatian loves to run and is an ideal coach dog. Diet guru Richard Simmons says of his six Dalmatians, 'Dalmatians are the court jesters of the dog world. They love to play, smile and laugh. They're like Bette Midler and Julia Roberts — real beauties with a sense of humor.'

The Keeshond, also known as 'the Dutch Barge Dog,' is an old breed from the Netherlands, where it once served as a guard dog and pet on the rijnaken or barges on the canals. In the late eighteenth century, the Keeshond was the symbol of the Patriots of Holland. When the House of Orange was restored to power, the Keeshond disappeared from the cities, but was still found in the countryside and along the waterways. It was once again popularized by the Baroness van Hardenbroek in the 1920s. Standing 17 to 18 inches tall, it looks like a large Pomeranian. Its coat is silver-gray with black-tipped hair. It is a hardy breed with a good disposition.

The Schipperke, or 'Skip,' is another 'barge dog' traditionally associated with the

Below and opposite: The Lhasa Apso is thought to have originated in the Himalayas. The name is derived from the name of the capital city of Tibet, Lhasa, and the Tibetan word meaning 'goat-like.'
Overleaf: *An engaging group of Shar-Peis. This breed may have also originated in the Himalayas.*

canals of Holland and Belgium. Although they originally guarded the canals and hurried the barge-pulling horses along, their popularity as pets soared after the Queen of Belgium acquired one. While its body looks much like a sled dog's, its face has a foxlike appearance, with a sharp nose that it sticks into every bit of the family's business. This active, black-coated fellow weighs between six and 18 pounds.

The Lhasa Apso — whose name is derived from that of the sacred Tibetan city of Lhasa — originated in Central Asia and is a very old breed. For centuries, only Tibetan nobility, lamas, dignitaries and high-ranking military officers were allowed to own Lhasa Apsos. The nobles and lamas kept a Mastiff outside their doors, but inside they kept at least one Lhasa Apso for protection. The very intelligent Lhasa Apso has a keen sense of hearing and an innate ability to distinguish friend from foe. They have a dense coat which varies in color from gold to black. While they look cuddly, they have a quick temper and are not the ideal pet for a busy child.

125